Gatherings for Greatness

24 Game-Changing Ingredients to Make Meetings the Secret Sauce of Your Success

ANA-MARIE JONES &
PORCIA CHEN SILVERBERG

AUTHOR
ACADEMY elite

Published by Author Academy Elite
P.O. Box 43, Powell, OH 43035

AuthorAcademyElite.com

Paperback ISBN: 978-1-64085-357-7

Hardcover ISBN: 978-1-64085-358-4

Ebook ISBN: 978-1-64085-359-1

Library of Congress Control Number: 2018907734

Dedicated to the conveners of meetings, the summoners of good

Dedication: To Our Heroes

We extend our deepest appreciation to all the caring souls who bring people together to create a better world. You—our conveners, connectors, and community builders—are our true heroes.

When everyday people step up to address a community need, they often become accidental community organizers. Others find themselves in the role of facilitator through their titles or positions at work. Still, others come to this role through their neighborhood or homeowners' associations, participation in civic groups such as Rotary Clubs or Elks Lodges, or their religious institutions.

No matter how you've come to the honored role of "summoner of good, convener of community," we tip our hats to you!

The most fulfilled people are those who get up every morning and stand for something larger than themselves.
—Wilma Mankiller, the first female chief of the Cherokee Nation

Table of Contents

*Change the way you look at things and
the things you look at will change.*
—*Wayne W. Dyer, author*

Introduction

Do you love going to meetings? No? We didn't think so. Meetings have a bad reputation. Everyone has their own pet peeves about meetings, and we do too. Some of our pet peeves will become obvious soon enough.

We are inviting you to change the way you look at meetings and claim them as the secret sauce behind your success. We are imploring you to ignore the countless books and articles devoted to slaying the meeting beast. Meetings are unfairly maligned and woefully misunderstood! From this point forward, we want to woo you into embracing meetings and other gatherings as a brilliant stage for dynamic human development, shared inspiration, interpersonal connections, and countless joyful moments.

This effort is not based on theory or wishful thinking run amok. We know it's possible to have uniquely meaningful meetings—we've done it. We've witnessed how casual gatherings can become moving and inspiring events. If you start with the solid foundation of having a good purpose for your meeting, the ideas in this book will help you and your chosen community fulfill your goals when those ideas are faithfully executed.

Before we get into the specifics of how to make meetings and other gatherings the secret sauce behind your success, we must acknowledge how challenging it can be to change how they are organized. We've seen how people become attached to running events the way they have always been run because change can be hard and threatening. The people tasked with making meetings happen don't often have the resources or authority needed to institute deep change. This is the feedback we've gotten, and it's what we've both experienced. We hear you. We've felt your pain and we're with you in the struggle.

We offer our ideas in the form of individual ingredients because meetings and other gatherings are as different and unique as the people who organize and attend them. Whether your meetings are one-on-one or have a few thousand participants, you can choose to add just a dash of one ingredient, or you can serve up something entirely new, using several of the more daring and unusual ingredients. It's up to you.

The *Gatherings for Greatness* ingredients will help make your meeting attendees hunger for more. When you're starting out, be selective in how you choose to infuse new flavors into your gatherings. Once you've cultivated an appetite for this approach, you can add more. If you're dealing with people who have more delicate sensibilities, you can start with the ingredients which change the ambient environment before trying to shift the basic recipe.

For many of your attendees, the addition of just one of these ingredients could make your meeting their must-attend event. However you need it to work, we are here to support you in being great while you convene your community to do great things.

Remember, when you host or attend meetings that feel like obligations or necessary evils to be avoided or tolerated, a spectacular opportunity is being wasted. Bringing people together to learn, grow, create, or better themselves and the world is a profoundly wonderful thing to do. Let's make that happen!

Can we assume you are ready to shake off the shackles holding back your meetings? Do you want to be known for having gatherings people truly *love* (gasp!) to attend? We hope so. Please, say yes, and read on.

Here's the ugly truth about meetings:

Meetings are not designed to be great experiences for the participants. Period.

It's true. They're not. If you can think of some exceptions, yay you! Most meetings, however, are held in service to some other process or project. Staff meetings are a classic example of a type of gathering not concerned with being great. These familiar staples are generally held in support of the proper and routine functioning of the office. Staff meetings are not envisioned, planned, nor delivered to infuse inspiration, cultivate a deeper sense of community, or help each participant to learn and grow. It's no wonder short meetings are universally applauded, meeting-free zones are appealing, and eye-rolling at the thought of some meetings is expected. Meeting hating is rampant, mediocre meetings are common, but you can change them. You should absolutely change them.

What would it mean to you and your people if your meetings and other gatherings became brilliant platforms for building and strengthening your communities?

Whenever you bring people together in a properly designed and delivered gathering, you have an unparalleled opportunity to build a stronger and more united society. You can choose to have your meetings help participants become more skilled and empowered in life, work, or community roles.

Everyone can benefit from better meetings and every person has a part to play in changing the status quo. It starts with insisting that the meetings and gatherings you fund, host, plan, facilitate, or participate in are structured for maximum participant benefit and engagement. Maximum PARTICIPANT benefit and engagement.

Some points in *Gatherings for Greatness* may seem simple or obvious, but they are here because they are so often omitted, and they are important.

We both have long histories as entrepreneurs, consultants, and nonprofit executive directors, so we've invested many thousands of hours in meetings. Only occasionally were these meetings mind-numbingly bad. Many were fine, but the majority were forgettable.

A precious few were brilliant, life-changing, and remarkable. We love those.

With this book in hand, you will be able to produce more engaging, meaningful, and time-effective meetings. You can use this content in the planning, delivery, and post-event debrief stages of any gathering where a key intention is to have greater participant engagement and satisfaction. We want to help you make your meetings matter more to *every* participant.

Our other wish for you is for you to cultivate your love for bringing people together, which should inspire you to seek more opportunities to do so. Here's to creating meetings that matter and making the world a better place!

Ana-Marie and Porcia

> *Mobilize others with radical*
> *acts of generosity.*
> —*Robyn Scott, author and social entrepreneur*

The Ingredients

You are defined by your ingredients,
by the way you touch them, by the flavors
you draw from them.
—Graham Elliot, Chef

The journey rarely begins the way you scripted.
—Brandi Chastain, Olympic gold medalist
soccer player

Ingredient: First Things First

L ifting your meetings and gatherings to new heights requires having a firm grasp of the basics. Before you start trying to add new and exciting bits and pieces to spice up your meetings, you need to give your existing protocols and standards a good review. By good review, we mean being objective, brutally honest, open-minded, and brave-hearted. It's necessary to do this right.

Conducting a thorough (line by line, piece by piece) review of your current meeting mindset and methods is especially important if the gatherings you seek to elevate involve a regular or familiar audience. First-time audiences, or audiences in which the people are only acquaintances or strangers to you, come with far fewer expectations and pitfalls. Recurring audiences are almost always the most important ones. They are your people, your posse, and your tribe. Whether it's your family, regular customers, association members, vendors, clients, consumers, partners, patrons, volunteers, or employees—however you refer to the people you regularly engage—make your gatherings truly meaningful for them and your world will change.

It's extra helpful to have a trusted confidant or two to help you review your meeting style, delivery, content, and planning processes. If your co-reviewers have attended one or more of your meetings, so much the better. They can give you needed feedback and an informed perspective. If there is a video of a meeting you've orchestrated, make it available to your feedback team. Empower them by making it safe for them to give you even painfully honest feedback.

So, what are you looking for in this deep review? Glad you asked! You are looking for a few specific aspects of how you plan and implement your gatherings.

1) How are you including participants? Are they part of the creation, planning, delivery, setup, and support?
2) Have you spoken to your people so they show up ready, able, and eager to

        address whatever needs to get done at the meeting or gathering?

3) Do you have a good sense of what your participants need for the meeting or gathering to be a real win for them?

4) How have you made it easy for attendees to participate — mentally, physically, professionally, socially, or emotionally — throughout the meeting or gathering? This requires understanding the needs of your participants at a deep level. For example, have you considered whether your crowd has introverts or others who would likely find group engagements more stressful? If yes, and if you are committed to ALL people feeling safe and being able to fully participate, then you'll need to include ways for them to easily opt out of certain activities, participate remotely, or take on some other role that is comfortable for them.

At the heart of making meetings great for the participants is seeing the world through their eyes and understanding their wants, needs, and aspirations.

There's a famous quote by Zig Ziglar: "You can have everything you want in life, if you will just help other people get what they want." When it comes to fully embracing the *Gatherings for Greatness* philosophy, this is true. Help people get what they truly need at your meetings and gatherings, and you will make miracles happen.

There are entire books on meeting planning and organizing, but recapping that same information is not the purpose of this book. For your convenience, we've included a link to some basic meeting checklists in the Resources section. So, if your own protocols are mainly in your head, or if they are so institutionalized it's hard to dissect the pieces, you can start with these lists.

Dropping your attachment to the way you've done things in the past is harder than it might look. Do it anyway.

The path to change is best traveled
when we travel together.
—Sheryl Sandberg,
Facebook Chief Operating Officer

This is the power of gathering: it inspires us, delightfully, to be more hopeful, more joyful, more thoughtful: in a word, more alive.
—Alice Waters, chef + restaurateur

Ingredient: Wisdom and Acceptance

No one sets out to have a bad, flat, or uninspiring gathering or meeting. They happen to good people and good organizations all the time. Here's a comforting bit of insight to hold onto: meetings are far more complex than they appear on the surface.

If you think it through, it becomes clear. The people needing the results are not necessarily the people with the skills or authority to plan and facilitate the meeting. The participants are often not a cohesive team with a shared vision for the outcome of the gathering. This is especially true for community engagement meetings where a diverse group of stakeholders come together to provide feedback in a public forum. Like most of humanity, neither the hosts nor the participants have been trained to see meetings as a platform for gathering, generating, and grooming greatness. Best practices aren't commonly shared. There is enough human turnover making continuity and institutional knowledge a challenge to maintain.

When we've asked participants what made a meeting special, memorable, or particularly meaningful for them, the answers were variations on the sentiments below:

- I felt heard. My experience mattered.
- It was interesting and engaging.
- Everyone was so positive.
- I felt proud/honored to be part of the group.
- My team learned things we can implement.
- I loved meeting and bonding with the other attendees.

This list is quite different from the list you get when you ask participants to evaluate a meeting. When you ask attendees to fill out evaluations for a meeting they felt went quite well, you often get comments like:

- Speakers were really good.
- The room was very nice.
- Registration went smoothly.
- Lunch was delicious.
- Wi-Fi worked!

It's possible to have a meeting with great components (wonderful speakers, beautiful location, excellent venue, delicious food, no major screw-ups, good Wi-Fi) where the attendees don't leave feeling energized, proud, or more excited to be more connected to each other.

Both of us have binders and Stuff We All Get (SWAG) from meetings that received very high marks on the evaluation forms for the speakers, venue, food, registration, etc. Neither of us cracked the spine of many of the binders we were given, nor did those meetings give us any new skills or perspectives, and we didn't leave with a greater sense of why we were there or what our roles were for the future.

Remember, these were some of the good meetings, conferences, or gatherings.

Embracing the essence of *Gatherings for Greatness* means success is measured and centered on what makes the experience great for the attendees and participants. Please reread that last sentence. The status quo has a strong gravitational pull and it's easier to default to the usual fare in life and in meetings.

Millions of people spend millions of hours in meetings. You have the power to make yours matter in ways that can change the world or you can make it mean the world to the people who attend. Many prominent issues facing humanity will take decades and millions of dollars to resolve. Some of the ideas in this book can be implemented for free and you could start at your next meeting. It is that simple.

If you are at the top of your business food chain and you are blessed with sufficient resources, you'll be able to readily implement any of these concepts. Your only potential obstacle will be your ability to genuinely enroll your team in the new possibilities you are striving to achieve.

For many more of you, however, it'll be more of a stretch. It'll require a sophisticated sales job to senior management or a board of directors. Or, perhaps, you'll need to get buy-in from several people and it may seem like a mountain to climb with many potential challenges. Even if it is so, it will still be worth it!

Whatever you face, remember to go forth with both wisdom and acceptance. There's no turning back once you see how great your meetings can be.

A key component of wisdom is fearlessness, which is not the absence of fear, but rather not letting our fears get in the way.
—Arianna Huffington, founder of
The Huffington Post

Plan your work, and work your plan.
—Pat Summitt, NCAA Basketball Coach

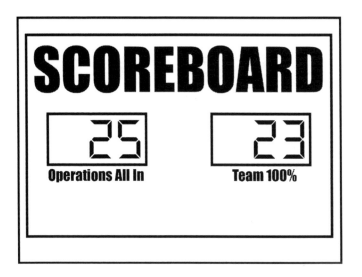

Ingredient: Naming,
Framing, and Gaming
Your Goal

Y ou are reading this book, so we assume you are committed to raising the bar for your meetings. To increase your chances of fulfilling the commitment, we highly recommend a 3-step process for goal-setting.

Step 1: Naming It

You get to decide what you want to achieve. Is it your goal to create a more bonded, connected, and aligned team? Do you want to ensure your attendees are 100% active at your meetings or events? Whatever it is, name it.

Make sure you and everyone on your implementation team can clearly articulate the goal and there is zero ambiguity as to what constitutes success.

Descriptive names to capture your aspirations are particularly useful, like "Operation All In" or "Team 100%." You should create something special for the implementation team and it could be a clever acronym. The important thing is for everyone to own it, know exactly what it means, and for them to be inspired to achieve it.

Step 2: Framing It

When you are creating your goals, sharing about them, or looking to see if they are on track, it's important to frame the conversations and actions around the heart and soul of the goals.

Use language and imagery that will resonate with your team as well as colors, cheers, music – anything that evokes strong positive feelings and inspires your tribe.

If you pick a goal of having 100% engagement in a process or project, it's important to have it framed around why 100% participation matters and why their 100% buy-in and engagement makes all the difference.

Without the proper and empowered framing, goals can sound and feel too random or disconnected from the heart of your shared vision.

Step 3: Gaming It

Even if you are a team of one taking on making your meetings matter, it helps to bring in the spirit of it being a worthy game. This step is about embracing the pursuit of the goal as a game. With the right attitude—win, lose, or draw—you will learn something from the game and the way you played it.

If you are engaging a team in your efforts to infuse the *Gatherings for Greatness* concepts, make it a real game with rules, guidelines, time limits, winners, and runners-up.

Going back to the 100% engagement example, you could make a game out of everyone on the team taking on some aspect of getting the participants to engage. Set time limits, appoint a referee, award points, create cheers and cheerleaders, and otherwise make it fun to be in active pursuit of such a worthy goal.

Imagine what a trade association or a chamber of commerce could accomplish if they set a goal of 100% engagement for their active members at their next gathering. How could that strengthen their organization? Having every person aligned, every person clear, and every action supporting the same goal would be remarkable. Imagine the results achieved, the relationships strengthened, the experiences gained, the records updated, and so much more!

Everything you are doing is in service to the greater goals you've set. The focus should always remain on those goals and how it benefits the people you seek to engage in your meetings and gatherings. *Name it. Frame it. Game it.*

If you project big goals, you may fall short, but you'll achieve more than you thought possible.
—*Theresa Grentz, basketball coach*

Who would refuse an invitation
to such a shining adventure?
—*Amelia Earhart, pioneer aviator*

Ingredient: The Invitation

F or many meetings, the prospective attendees aren't graciously or personally invited
to attend. From staff meetings to homeowners'
associations meetings to major conferences,
the would-be participants are likely simply notified of the event and encouraged to
RSVP. The invite is made with an unspoken
understanding, and it's not truly a personal
communication to the receiver.

Isn't it easy to skip an event when it appears
it's not important that you personally attend?
Now, of course, we are not suggesting you
hand write a formal personal invitation to
each person on your mailing list. We're rather
extreme about wanting meetings to be brilliant, but we're realistic. You can do better
than notifying your desired attendees and
asking for their registration (we're picturing
you nodding in agreement).

With the magic of mass mailings and email
distribution services, you can send out personalized advance notification about the event to
your VIPs, followed by a save-the-date notice,

and then send a personalized note expressing why you hope he or she will attend—making sure to include details of special interest to the receiver. If resources allow, you can raise the bar on your invitations by placing some personal phone calls to extend an invitation and request their attendance.

With personalized invitations and phone calls, you can hyper-tailor your message to address the most unique needs of your individual attendees. If it's not obvious that your meeting content and logistics will expressly address the interests of participants whose key issues aren't traditionally included, the personalized invitations and phone calls are the place to make it happen. This gesture could be especially meaningful to people with disabilities, individuals with language barriers, members of your LGBTQIA (Lesbian, Gay, Bisexual, Transgender, Queer, Intersex, Allied) community, or anyone else who needs meetings to be more meaningful and valuable.

Long before your key potential attendees see the generic invite, you can make certain they know how valued they are, how much you hope to see them, and why it would make a difference for them to attend your meeting. Personal phone calls can more than double meeting attendance.

As an added benefit, in our experience, people who were called were far more diligent about notifying the organizer if they were going to be late or if they needed to cancel. The invitation was no longer generic, it was personal, and people responded in kind.

For meetings that are open to the public, make sure the invite information removes any barriers to attendance. Consider including more detailed information in the invite or registration confirmation:

- Time
- Date
- Exact location (including building name, floor, and room)

- Map
- Parking options
- Public transit info and links to the facility
- Reminder to bring business cards
- Information on food or other offerings
- Any available services or accommodations (American Sign Language translators, assistive hearing devices, shuttle services, etc.)
- Reminder to come prepared to share a practiced 15-second introduction. (Even if you don't have dedicated time on the agenda for everyone to introduce themselves, encourage everyone to practice a 15-second introduction. Many meetings and social gatherings would be significantly improved if everyone came with a good, short, powerful introduction.)

The invitation is often the first tangible representation of the meeting a would-be attendee experiences. Make it gracious, personal, engaging, informative, and compelling. If your targeted participant wants to attend, it should be easy to register, find out more information, and arrive ready and eager to make the most of the experience.

> *Nothing annoys people so much*
> *as not receiving invitations.*
> —*Oscar Wilde, poet + playwright*

The ideal space must contain elements of magic,
serenity, sorcery, and mystery.
—Luis Barragan, architect

Ingredient: Physical
Environment

Look around your meeting space. Does it add power to your vision, goals, and aspirations? Take your time. We'll wait.

Did you discover your meeting room looks too basic? It may be an awesome room, but does the space shout your vision and help people fully engage in your shared aspirations? Most meeting rooms don't, but you can change them.

If you can't select an ideal space for your meeting, you may have to bust out your MacGyver problem-solving skills to make the space better serve your attendees. Rolling partitions, curtains, and shoji screens can help create a more private and defined space. Strategic positioning of dry-erase sheets and flipcharts on easels can allow for note capturing and facilitation in a non-standard room.

The more you know about the needs of your attendees, the easier it will be to make the environment supportive of the meeting activities. It is critical to collect this information as part of the registration process and to ensure your chosen space is not only ADA compliant, but also set up and maintained to allow full and unencumbered access by people using walkers, wheelchairs, scooters, and other mobility aids. This is true whether or not any of your attendees self-identify as disabled or use these devices.

If you have the chance to hold a meeting in a space specifically designed to support people with disabilities, we highly recommend jumping on the opportunity. The wider doorways and hallways, movable walls, built-in technology, and ample lifts and ramps allow for flow, flexibility, and customized setup, thus allowing for a superior experience for all participants. Having ample space for attendees to move freely and to easily set up and display poster boards, flip charts, and props, is an added blessing to the success of any meeting.

No matter where you hold your meetings and gatherings, it's an important and worthy investment to do whatever you can to have the physical space support the participants in fully immersing themselves in the content, spirit, and purpose of your meeting.

This is especially true when the participants are engaging in a topic not native to them or when it's a small part of their consciousness. The environment you create can help your audience remember why they care, refresh their understandings of the specifics of your past meetings, and otherwise stay more focused on the subject.

For example, both of us have hosted numerous meetings where the topic was emergency preparedness, disaster response, or community continuity. The people in the audience were often far removed from traditional emergency management positions. For many of our attendees, the language and imagery of emergency management were both difficult and unrelated to their day jobs and positions. It is much more important for people to have the visual cues, reminders, and tools when it's not a familiar conversation.

Some of the low-hanging fruit in making the physical environment support the participants includes:

- Props
- Posters
- Signs
- Placemats
- Costumes
- Water bottle wrappers
- PowerPoint presentations
- Handouts
- Photos
- Memorabilia
- Video clips
- Wearable SWAG

To give a presentation to a friend's employees, Ana-Marie dressed in full costume as her preparedness alter-ego, Ms. Duct Tape (@ MsDuctTape online). Her friend, Cate Steane, came as her alter-ego, Safety Freak, to co-present a preparedness training to her employees. It is safe to say the participants remember the presentation well—and, not just for the fun content and interactive presentation style. The visuals of seeing your boss in a head-to-toe colorful costume, decked out with safety items, interacting with MsDuctTape (who wears a duct tape mask, cape, tools, and lots of safety accessories) is quite sticky and hard to forget.

For a board of directors strategic planning meeting, Porcia was inspired to print out some of the recent high-praise and generous comments her nonprofit consumers shared. She posted these comments on the walls all around the meeting room before the meeting started. Porcia also invited board members to walk around the room reading the testimonials before the meeting formally began and during breaks.

Comments included members' appreciation of the organization's leadership development programs, how much their organization had benefited from greater collaborations with colleagues because of past gatherings, and how they had increased their donor and volunteer base because of contacts made at meetings the organization hosted.

The visuals of seeing a roomful of glowing and enthusiastic praise from their colleagues and respected community leaders about the organization they chose to serve as a board leader were validating. It was a timely reminder of why everyone was at this strategic planning meeting and why they were in business. More importantly, it was an opportunity to feel the pride of being affiliated with an esteemed organization, validating their own wisdom in investing their energy in a worthy cause, and they feasted on the knowledge that they were part of something great.

Help your attendees stay engaged throughout meetings by making your physical space speak your vision, passion, and goals ... without uttering a word aloud.

Architecture can't force people to connect, it can only plan the crossing pointes, remove barriers, and make the meeting places useful and attractive.
—Denise Scott Brown, Architect

There's always room for a story that can transport people to another place.
—J.K. Rowling, author and screenwriter

Ingredient: Stories and Memorable Moments

More than facts, figures, or dazzling PowerPoint presentations, people remember stories. Powerful, true, and relevant stories can bring an audience to tears, fits of laughter, or a new understanding of an issue or opportunity. Meetings featuring stories, and memorable moments to become future stories, are meetings people love to experience and hate to miss.

Storytelling is an art form and it can be learned. If it's possible, support at least a few people from your team in becoming skilled storytellers. There are workshops, books, TED Talks, and YouTube videos, just to name a few reliable resources to help your team develop their storytelling chops. Building a diverse cadre of skilled storytellers is helpful because people will listen differently depending on the storyteller's age, gender, ethnicity, ability, title, seniority, and so on. Beyond the ways they will benefit your own meetings, confident and engaging storytellers are offered opportunities for public speaking, training, video segments, and more.

The number of topics you can cover in stories is endless. Some examples:

- The history of your group or company
- The personal story of the founder
- The difference made by the group or company
- The personal connection of the storyteller to the group or company
- The story of a customer, client, or person served by the group or company
- The way your group or company is addressing a big or critical issue
- The proudest, happiest, most meaningful, or most important moment for the group or company

The list goes on. Capturing memorable moments and turning them into compelling stories shared in your extended community is a habit worth cultivating.

A memorable moment for Porcia happened the first time Ana-Marie presented a keynote at Porcia's organization's annual conference. Porcia gave a gushing and sincere introduction of Ana-Marie, who then took the stage. Instead of launching into her presentation, Ana-Marie turned to Porcia to acknowledge her contribution to the region, leadership of the social sector, commitment to preparedness for vulnerable people, and collaborative spirit in their respective organizations' partnership. Ana-Marie invited the audience to join her in recognizing Porcia's contributions. The meeting attendees responded with thunderous applause, hooting, and loud cheering.

To say Porcia was caught off guard by Ana-Marie's generous and elegant acknowledgment is an understatement. She didn't expect a presenter to thank the conference host, nor was she prepared to be recognized so profoundly by someone she respected in front of high-level dignitaries, respected leaders, and colleagues.

The energy in the room shifted dramatically as the rush of dopamine swept through the crowd. The smiles, increased enthusiasm, and emotional high carried over throughout the day. The level of trust and friendship between the two of us blossomed to a new level after this memorable moment.

If you can tell a story well, you can move people to do something.
— *Soledad O'Brien, broadcast journalist*

In acknowledgment of our past, we become
strengthened to embrace our future.
—Eleesha, author

Ingredient: Acknowledgment

If you ask a roomful of people how many of them are tired of being acknowledged for their efforts and contributions, you won't find many hands raised. All of us hunger for confirmation our actions and efforts make a difference, yet we seldom get enough of this reassurance. In too many fields, a subset of participants toil away in a chronic state of acknowledgment deprivation.

You can use meetings as an opportunity to address the chronic problem of acknowledgment deprivation by adding time to your agenda to give these people the recognition they need and deserve. Just two minutes near the opening of your meeting can energize and inspire participants. The sense of accomplishment coming from being genuinely acknowledged inspires people to continue doing their best and more than justifies the tiny investment in time.

Recognition and acknowledgment matter. A powerfully delivered and heartfelt acknowledgment can help restore self-esteem and renew passion and commitment. Done well, acknowledgment revives the spirit and lifts the soul.

A generous use of meeting time is to deeply acknowledge people for the contributions they make. It's meaningful to acknowledge those whose efforts often go unseen and unheralded, but without which the project, event, or undertaking would not succeed.

An easy example comes from the field of emergency management. When firefighters rescue people from a burning building, they are heroes. Period. We heap thanks and praise upon them for their obvious bravery. Both children and adults wave and cheer as the fire engines go by. The profession is regarded as "America's bravest," and the newest, greenest firefighter instantly becomes a member of a loved and admired tribe.

If, however, you are committed to emergency preparedness, don't hold your breath waiting for any praise. You can fight the long uphill battle of helping people make themselves and their communities safer and better able to respond to crises, but you won't get any validation or love. You will, however, be expected to do your preparedness work for free, without resources, and without taking time away from your daily routines.

How about some name calling? Detractors call people with a passion for preparedness doomsday preppers, worrywarts, bureaucrats, and other less-than-empowering names. Is it any wonder preparedness aficionados often exist in an almost total dearth of acknowledgment? Bringing public acknowledgment to this group has been an emotionally moving and eye-opening experience for both of us. Many people in our audiences had never been acknowledged for their preparedness work. This was true not only for volunteer community readiness advocates, but also for professional emergency managers. Several of them said that being acknowledged this way was the first time they felt their efforts in preparedness were truly appreciated.

Acknowledging Groups

It is easy and fast to publicly acknowledge groups of people in worthwhile ways at a large meeting. You've likely attended events in which much time and effort was taken to acknowledge elected officials, honored guests, and sponsors. There are other entire groups who can and should be acknowledged in certain meetings.

Which group should we choose as our example? Nonprofits, of course! Why? Because they deserve it. Too often, the work of these unsung heroes is overlooked, and if using nonprofits as an example inspires some of you to recognize them in your meetings, we'll be over-the-moon delighted.

Here's a process we found successful. The facilitator asks the audience to show appreciation of this special group of people by both listening attentively and joining in the recognition with applause and cheers. It doesn't matter if your staff members are paid or volunteer, are in their first week or have logged fifty years, or are board members or the lowest-level newbie employee. Once they are standing and you have a quiet and focused room, lavish sincere words of appreciation on them.

Not sure what to say? The following statements have been quite meaningful to many of our nonprofit partners:

> We want to bring special recognition to you, our nonprofit friends and partners. Some of the greatest challenges in our world—ending homelessness, stopping domestic violence, addressing climate change, protecting our most vulnerable people, curing cancer and other deadly diseases—are the challenges you take on every single day. You are the community change-agents, the tireless champions for the common good and for equality. Everyone here benefits from what you do because your work helps to create a better world. No group is consistently asked to do more with less than you. While you don't wear capes, we recognize you are

clearly our superheroes. Thank you so much for what you do and for being with us today.

It takes less than forty-five seconds to say those words. Add another ninety seconds for the time it takes to get the honorees to stand, a period of thunderous applause, and the time it takes to sit back down, and you've served up a successful acknowledgment that makes people feel valued in under two minutes.

Two minutes.

We want to see much more recognition given to nonprofits and other groups who have made a positive difference. Some of you are starting from zero recognition time on your agendas. Setting aside two minutes is an easy goal and this tiny time investment will provide huge dividends. Depending on the length and nature of your meeting, you can add individual names, specific accomplishments, more nuanced recognition of achievements, and a presentation of awards or certificates.

The setup for a more specific acknowledgment is simple. The person being acknowledged is called by name and asked to stand or come to the podium. The speaker looks directly at this person while describing his or her contributions. Ideally, the person delivering the acknowledgment should be someone the receiver will be honored to hear speak about their efforts. Sometimes it's someone the receiver knows; sometimes it is someone well known in the community or an authority figure. It could be a celebrity or someone who may be unknown but is particularly adept at giving acknowledgments.

The speaker is not simply thanking a person for doing something. She is acknowledging *why* this person's actions mattered, *what* was made possible because of those actions, and *how* this person made a real difference to you, the group, the company, or the cause. Generosity and sincerity are key when giving acknowledgment.

If called to the podium, the honoree is presented with a certificate or another token of appreciation before returning to her or his seat, all the while basking in sounds of praise.

A Group Effort

The whole room can help make this acknowledgment moment more special and memorable for the receiver. First, they can listen intently (simply asking the audience to do this works very well). All the people in the room can also help by affirming their support with applause, cheers, or other signs of validation. Finally, audience members can later offer their own words, gestures, or gifts. In this way, everyone present at the meeting becomes a participant in recognizing the honoree and sharing in the good energy resulting from acknowledgment.

Acknowledge generously, with nuance, detail, and sincerity. Give people their full moment in the sun and help them take it all in.

There are two things people want more than sex and money—recognition and praise.
—Mary Kay Ash, founder of Mary Kay Cosmetics

Networking is more about "farming" than it is "hunting." It's about cultivating relationships.
—Dr. Ivan Misner, founder of BNI

Ingredient: Networking to Build a Better World

Don't make any assumption when you see the first word in this ingredient. We are NOT recommending your grandfather's model of business networking. Traditional networking, where the main purpose is to expand your business network, get new clients and sales, and build a quality referral relationship, certainly has its place. It's not here. This type of networking fails to deliver what's needed most when you embrace the *Gatherings for Greatness* philosophy.

In this community, we prize and seek interaction over transaction, and our unwavering focus remains on what builds, bonds, and betters the people at our meetings and gatherings. If your team is seeking to transform an industry, coalesce around a cause, or otherwise take on a great goal, some skills are indispensable. Thankfully, they can be learned and honed with different types of engagement exercises. For example, easily relating to diverse people with different beliefs, and then quickly (under 10 minutes) finding common ground are brilliant skills to cultivate.

Below is an example of an exercise which never fails to produce positive results when properly facilitated. It's best with at least 15 people in attendance and when you have a minimum of 10 minutes for a group engagement.

Oh, Me Three!

In this exercise, you split the attendees into groups of three. It's important the groups are made up of three people—not two or four—three people. You are going to set them free and task them with actively finding points of agreement and common ground.

Each group of three picks someone to be the scribe, writing down what ALL THREE people have in common. The person to the right of the scribe starts with a simple statement or question:

> I have a dog.
> I'm allergic to shellfish.
> I've traveled to all 50 states.
> I love volunteering at a homeless shelter.
> Who else LOVES Game of Thrones?

Can you juggle?

Do you have siblings?

Items only get included on the list if all three people have this in common. This exercise isn't about simply agreeing and creating the longest list. Each person can decide to use questions or statements to elicit answers from the other two group members. The structure isn't important; achieving the goal of finding true common ground is what matters. Participants can also build off each other's comments.

For example, if someone mentions a love of dogs, IF ALL AGREE they all love dogs, they can then ask about favorite breeds. Through questions, statements, and dialogue they could discover everyone in the group loves small dogs and they all had a dog named Oreo.

The facilitator should instruct the group to not pick the obvious and easily observable common points, like "we all have brown hair." If a random person could notice the common ground in passing, it's not something to be added to the list.

When I (Ana-Marie) facilitate this exercise I often start by asking everyone in the room three questions. Who loves dogs? Who loves coffee ice cream? Who has a younger sister? Then, I ask who said "yes" to all three questions. At a large meeting, I had several hands raised. So, I asked if any of them had a younger sister named Lisa. In under two minutes, in a large conference room, I found three people who share my love of dogs and coffee ice cream, and we all have younger sisters named Lisa.

This exercise consistently produces AMAZING results. One group of three random people discovered they all did missionary work in the same African village, but in different decades. Another group of women of three different generations all married—and divorced—their high school sweethearts. Levels of detail and nuance are revealed in as little as five to seven minutes. It creates a bond.

When the timer goes off, the facilitator has each group tally how many points of common ground they found. The groups call out their "Oh, Me Three!" scores and the ones with the lowest and highest numbers read aloud their answers. Sometimes the longest list is filled with generic items—we all like to read, we all live in this county, we all drove to this meeting. At other times, the short list will have greater nuance and intimate details—we all have blended families, we all survived cancer, we all still love our jobs after over 25 years. Once in a blue moon, a group will struggle to find any common points, and they still marvel at how great it was to discover so much about each other so quickly.

If a group is particularly animated during the exercise, we have them share the source. At a meeting held in a community room in a police station in Concord, California, the three youngest attendees at a community pre-paredness meeting became a group. They were all in their late teens or early twenties and they didn't know each other. They broke out laughing constantly during the five minutes they were tasked to find common ground. It was quite noticeable, so we asked what was so funny.

They were still laughing as they shared they all had the same thoughts during the exercise. None of the group members thought they'd ever hear themselves say, "We are in a police station. We are not under arrest. We are not in trouble. We are having a good time. We'd come back!"

If your goal is to have a more bonded team, a genuinely connected community, or to empower every team member's confidence by interacting with other team members, then this type of engagement exercise and framing can make all the difference.

Lindsay Fox, an Australian entrepreneur, said "personal relationships are always the key to good business. You can buy networking; you can't buy friendships." We couldn't agree more. Forming business friendships and meaningful alliances takes effort for most people. Left to their own devices, many people will sit with the same people, in the same place in the room, and engage in the same types of conversations they usually have with their colleagues and fellow meeting denizens.

A very simple (but incredibly useful) thing to do is have people ask each other questions. You can have them partner with someone entirely unknown to them or you can pair them up with the people surrounding them. The goal is to spur happy and different banter. That's it.

This can happen before the meeting, during breaks, or while standing in line. By providing questions and encouraging attendees to ask these questions, you are taking away barriers, helping to peel people away from their cell phones and devices, and you are making it easy for people to avoid uncomfortable issues.

These questions can inspire your attendees to be more prosocial. Some people are not skilled conversationalists, sometimes there are other barriers or impediments, and it's painful or awkward for some to try to engage on their own.

The questions below are easy, require more than a one-word reply, and inspire participants to learn a bit about each other in a safe and non-threatening manner.

You can create your own custom list of questions and you can give people time to share what they've learned about each other if the timing and energy are right.

1. How would you spend six hours with a close friend?
2. What is your favorite movie/documentary? Why?
3. If you wrote a book about your life, what would the title be? Why?
4. What has been one of your happiest or proudest moments? Why?

5. Name three things you are thankful for right now in life.

6. What lesson did you have to learn the hard way? How can you help others avoid the same experience?

7. What are three of your favorite ways to relax, rejuvenate, and reconnect?

8. What's an interesting fact about you most people don't know?

9. If you could study with any expert in the world, who would you work with and what would you study?

10. What's your favorite pizza topping? Who makes your favorite pizza?

If you have more time, or if extra time unexpectedly opens in your agenda, a skilled facilitator can turn these simple questions into a more involved exercise where the whole room learns more about each other.

Most of the greatest relationships in your life started with a simple conversation. Be the conversation starter. Embrace Sylvia Plath's thinking: "I love people. Everybody. I love them, I think, as a stamp collector loves his collection. Every story, every incident, every bit of conversation is raw material for me." Find the exercises and questions that will open the hearts and minds of your community.

Remember, just as meetings were never designed to be great for the participants, old-school networking exercises were not intended to create the results we seek here. Be patient if you have to overcome resistance to participation. As beneficial as our clients have found our different approach to network-ing to be, several initially needed convincing because many have a negative association with networking. Our most civic-minded part-ners, many of whom self-identify as being change-makers and catalysts for the public good, often recoiled from the overt salesy aspect of traditional networking. Others felt too introverted to willingly put themselves in classic networking environments. Some just felt it was too disconnected from their more communal goals and aspirations.

Help your tribe see "networking" time can be reworked so it truly helps them achieve their greater goals and aspirations.

It's important to find your tribe.
—RuPaul, actor + television personality

Give and give again. Keep hoping,
keep trying, keep giving!
— *Anne Frank, Holocaust diarist*

Ingredient: Rewards, Giveaways, and Sponsored Opportunities

A fine way to create energy, excitement, and enthusiasm in a room is to liberally sprinkle rewards, giveaways, and prizes throughout the meeting. This can be an excellent way to include sponsor opportunities for vendors and partners.

This engagement technique is useful when the content of the meeting is heavy, or less than sparkling. Sometimes mandatory compliance presentations delivered by unskilled vendors can be an energy drain. Other material is occasionally just more difficult to process—says Ana-Marie, nodding hard as she remembers some presentations on smallpox and refrigerated trucks for storing deceased disaster victims.

Especially in these cases, it's a delightful and useful mental break to have a two-minute interlude to answer a trivia question, solve a riddle, play a game, or win a raffle prize. Some companies look for places to demonstrate their products and giving them two minutes in front of the room in exchange for some prize is worth it to them.

Rewards, giveaways, and a sponsorship opportunity can also be combined for greater impact. Pacific Gas and Electric Company (PG&E) supports community preparedness and safety efforts. For a charity fundraiser for a nonprofit called Collaborating Agencies Responding to Disasters (CARD) they provided some financial support, and some preparedness SWAG in the form of keychain flashlights.

The event was a charity Texas Hold'em poker tournament. All the entrants received flashlights, and other safety SWAG was added to create special prizes to be given out if an eight and two aces appeared on the board. This was done to highlight and educate everyone on 8-1-1—a free phone line for any PG&E customer to call before beginning any type of digging project to help avoid safety hazards. The flashlights were used to teach participants about the safety code and the many ways to make small flashlights extra helpful in a crisis.

People who came out to support a safety organization got some safety SWAG, learned some whistle safety skills, cheered wildly when aces and eights appeared on the board, and they all learned about a PG&E safety-related phone number in the process.

You can get creative with your prizes in the event you don't have the budget for prizes or gift cards or if you don't have the time or inclination to request items from partners and vendors.

Some creative company gifts we like to suggest:

- A pass to wear casual clothes or be out of the official uniform at work
- A certificate allowing the bearer to choose the pizza toppings or the lunch destination
- A certificate to choose the music station
- Gift of a prized parking spot for a month
- A recognition statue or award that signifies exemplary work (rotated monthly or quarterly)
- Breakfast or lunch with the boss

- Choice of office charitable project or community service act

It helps to have someone with a real flair be the emcee to do the quick break and award the prizes. If it's done well, offering rewards, gifts, prizes, and giveaways at meetings and gatherings can be fun, uplifting, and physically energizing. It also provides a nice change of mental focus.

Every gift which is given, even though it be small, is in reality great if it is given with affection.
—Pindar, ancient Greek lyric poet

Just like we planned it, just like we practiced.
We did it.
—Alice Bowman, Mission Operations Manager
for the New Horizons mission to Pluto

Ingredient: Pre-meeting Huddles and Trainings

If executed faithfully, just about every other ingredient shared in this book will bring an obvious change in actions and experiences for your participants. Whether it's the sudden increase in interactivity, the addition of music, having an agenda with time allotted for wellness, or the new inclusion of signage, posters, and visual aids—regular attendees will know this meeting is not like the others.

This ingredient—instituting pre-meeting huddles and trainings—is about eliminating points of failure and ensuring everyone involved in the meeting production is on track, aligned, and firmly on the same up-to-the-minute updated page about the event.

It's hard to convey how much it means to the meeting production team to have this level of clarity, cohesion, and support to deliver an excellent event.

With the advent of smartphones, many of the issues related to communicating and sharing information have become non-issues. For every role at the event, there can be a shareable clear checklist. It's easy to take a short video to show a key procedure. Registration at an event can grind to a halt, all for want of a simple video on how to reload the new label printer. One A/V tech out sick can derail an entire conference.

Everyone should be trained on the function he or she will perform at the event, have the checklist for the position in print, and in soft digital on their smartphone. The instructions should be written so a reasonably intelligent person with a reasonable level of commitment could step in if someone is a no-show. Too much detail and it becomes unwieldy and confusing. Too little information and it's not a valuable tool.

Creating a text group on a shared app on every team member's smartphone will allow you to do a fast check-in, provide immediate updates, and keep everyone connected.

Before the event, the whole production team should be logged on to the Wi-Fi network at the event and have the backups they need pre-loaded. It helps to have at least one person check in directly with every member of the production team and ensure everyone is fully connected to the app and the whole team. Team members should also have each other's phone numbers programmed in their phones. For some events, we've had app connectivity, a text group, and an email group at the ready, and everyone was clear on the order to use them if a failure occurred.

Building in this level of tech connection and communication will allow you to hold a virtual check-in, eliminate the need for a face-to-face meeting during the event, and if someone is not at their best—or has an emergency—the whole team can quickly communicate and adjust.

The last in-person huddle should give everyone the opportunity to raise issues, share key changes, smooth out any last-minute concerns, and reaffirm the commitment to making this an incredible gathering for the people attending.

We know this section, for most people, isn't the cool new sexy fun thing, and we know it's positively steeped in our shared emergency resilience awareness. Because this ingredient is deployed behind the scenes, it's unlikely to result in the same type of gushing comments on the evaluations as you get when networking exercises, interactivity, and acknowledgments are part of the event.

This is about all members of the production team being trained, empowered, and ready to do their best—while knowing they are connected to a team, where everyone has each other's back.

With adequate planning, passion, and perseverance, you can achieve the God-given goals.
—Lailah Gifty Akita, founder of Smart Youth Volunteers Foundation

You only exist because of the agreements you made with yourself and with the other humans around you.
—José Luis Ruiz, author

Ingredient: Agreements and Ground Rules

Out of the many hundreds of meetings, gatherings, and engagements we've attended, it's a rare thing for the hosts to present the attendees with participation agreements and ground rules. This is a missed opportunity for some groups.

Beyond establishing shared standards and codes of behavior, it is in your agreements and ground rules where you can best lay the foundation for managing participant expectations. Civic gatherings, town hall meetings, and other public engagement experiences often struggle and devolve from the lack of clearly articulated and dynamically managed expectations.

One group we've both enjoyed presents all participants with a list of agreements to sign. Most of the agreements govern personal behaviors. The most memorable one involved all participants agreeing to make any complaints only to the people who can do something about the issue and you agree to not receive complaints unless you are the appropriate person to address it. This one agreement, for some people, was worth the price of admission to the whole course.

Imagine the positive environment you create when people don't walk around randomly looking to find the next ear to whine, moan, and complain to about something. Some people are a complaint waiting to happen, and they will happily, eagerly, share a random ranting complaint with anybody and everybody. Having an agreement cuts much of that out, and it gives everyone the ability to honor their promise to not receive complaints when they aren't empowered to address them.

For most meetings, organizers would be quite hesitant to require a signed agreement and for some meetings, it would be considered too formal. For some groups, or for certain types of multi-day retreats, a written and signed agreement can provide a strong framework to help attendees maintain personal best practices.

We highly recommend having the audience agree to some agreements and ground rules.

This can all be done from the podium in an upbeat and friendly manner. Clearly, the agreement and ground rules differ based on the facility. Convention centers, company offices, private yachts, and campgrounds each need to cover different issues in their agreements and rules.

As facilitators, we often have simple agreements and ground rules to cover how to help maintain a positive, productive, and safe learning environment.

Some basic agreements and ground rules include:

- You agree to not share personal or identifying information about other participants without their permission.
- You agree to answer the questions posed.
- You agree to help forward the agenda.
- You agree to return all borrowed tools and equipment.

When Ana-Marie facilitates or keynotes a large gathering of several hundred people or more, she often asks for everyone to set their phones on silent or vibrate. If a phone rings during the event, the offender agrees to pay a dollar and the audience is urged to encourage them to pay. It's awesome when a phone rings and hundreds of people let out an audible "whoop" to make the offender pay up. It turns a potentially disruptive or irritating moment into a fun exchange for the whole room.

A few simple, but highly effective, ways to have agreements and ground rules shared with your audience, beyond including them in your outreach and confirmation email:

1) Display your agreements as a PowerPoint slide cycling through with other useful info such as emergency numbers, reminders about meals, transit options, etc. The PowerPoint can play before the meeting and during breaks and meals.
2) Print your agreements and ground rules on the back of the agenda.

3) Post them in restroom stalls and wherever people congregate (coffee area, water fountain, elevator, etc.).

If ground rules are important enough to create, they are important enough to share, and they need to be seen by all.

WARNING! DO NOT go overboard with ground rules and agreements. It will irritate your attendees. Too much of this ingredient and all you'll taste is regret when you end up knee-deep in petty enforcement issues. Any agreements or ground rules you establish should help provide structure and eliminate sources of potential upset or breakdown.

If your meeting or gathering discusses sensitive topics, it's helpful to share agreements and ground rules in the spirit of keeping the space safe and welcoming to all.

Safety-related ground rules and agreements should help everyone feel protected, and to avoid accidents and emergencies.

You can create agreements and ground rules around any issue where the absence of guidance or lack of a shared understanding is likely to cause issues. Social media and technology use are notable examples where some agreements and ground rules are often needed.

Gatherings without proper safeguards, where everyone has an Internet connection, access to technology and social media platforms, pose a threat to your privacy needs, standards, and values. Phone, drone, recorder, and social media use at your meetings, without a shared understanding of the sensitive issues and consequences, is a recipe for grief and headaches. Agreements and ground rules can provide some relief.

The skillful and sensitive inclusion of technology can transform a meeting or gathering. It allows people with disabilities to fully participate. Participants anywhere in the world will also be allowed to join in. Technology can also revolutionize the whole registration and check-in process. Text polling technology can allow a level of immediate feedback and engagement to wow and engage your audience.

Building technology training into a meeting can leave everyone more connected, informed, and resilient just by participating. Gratuitous or careless use of technology is a nightmare and it can increase your potential points of failure exponentially.

There is so much we could say about social media use at meetings and gatherings. The pro vs. con list is very long. There are so many books, magazines, publications, podcasts, webinars, and videos about using social media, but we are not opening an enormously complex topic here. Google "social media success stories" and "social media failures" and you'll understand why we are both personally strongly pro-social media AND we believe it needs to be used with quality guidance, sensitivity, and care.

Having the extra structure of a written agreement and ground rules related to technology and social media use can provide welcomed guidance and it can help technology and social media to be extraordinary additions to your meetings or gatherings.

Remember to give thanks to everyone for agreeing to whatever requests you make of them in your agreements and ground rules.

Your life works to the degree
you keep your agreements.
—Werner Erhard, author + founder of
The est Training

It's a transformative experience to simply pause instead of immediately filling up the space.
—Pema Chodron, nun + American Tibetan Buddhist

Ingredient: Stillness and Movement

Most people live with both a great need for more stillness and a great need for more movement. Intentionally bringing both these elements to your meetings can have a remarkable impact.

Stillness

Many of us have schedules so packed with meetings and obligations we are rushing from one appointment to the next, sometimes for days at a time. While your meeting or gathering is critically important to you, for others it's just one of many commitments. Giving everyone an opportunity to have absolute silence and a brief escape from all forms of chatter, noise, and sounds is memorable.

Graciously invite your attendees to sit still, close their eyes, take some deep breaths, clear their thoughts, set an intention, and open their eyes with a new level of clarity and focus.

If your participants have to brave terrible traffic to get to you, if there are some tensions or discombobulating events, stillness and silence can be the antidote that resets the energy of the room.

For many people, the silent interlude you provide may be the first time they've been supported in slowing down enough to hear themselves think. Quiet time may seem foreign to some people, but its addition to meeting agendas has some surprisingly strong champions, including the so-called "Type A" folks from highly competitive industries. This makes a stronger case to deliberately include stillness in your meeting.

Movement

Just as stillness is the antidote to stressed brains and frenetic activity, movement is the antidote to the physical drains of meeting life. Health experts say sitting is the new smoking, and most meetings involve a lot of sitting. Your meetings can create movement to shift that.

A highly rated component of several meetings we've facilitated is time allotted for a wellness timeout. If your meeting lasts more than an hour, adding movement will help your attendees feel better. Providing short breaks (one to five minutes) where you add movement to support health and wellness can be a game changer. The range of activities include:

- Closing eyes, do slow intentional breathing, while gently tensing targeted muscles
- Slow and gentle rolling of shoulders and neck
- Standing up to do any of the above activities
- Doing some gentle yoga-like stretches
- Marching in place
- Walking around the room or area

It's important to make an open invitation to participate in welcoming wellness with movement and to provide a diverse variety of possible movements (like the list above) to ensure your invitation is appropriate and accessible to people with all levels of abilities and disabilities.

For longer meetings and multi-day events, you can engage members of the audience to help support this level of commitment to wellness. At the start of the meeting, ask if anyone in the audience practices yoga, meditation, Tai Chi, Reiki, or martial arts. Encourage them to champion the participants taking mini wellness breaks throughout the event.

Having participants stop periodically to breathe deeply or stand and stretch has left people feeling energized rather than stiff or tired after an all-day meeting. *If* the layout and design of the room allows for people to move freely without disturbing or distracting other participants, encourage people to move to the back of the room if they need to stretch or move to keep themselves comfortable and pain-free.

For groups where everyone feels comfortable standing, having a short meeting without sitting is a type of wellness activity. Other groups have brought in big balloons or inflated beach balls to give people the opportunity to move about, while some simply bounce a beach ball around the room.

Helping your attendees attend to their mental, physical, and emotional needs and comforts through both stillness and movement translates into much happier humans who feel better at the end of your meeting or gathering.

Your stillness and wellness moments present great opportunities to include members of your extended communities in your meeting and gatherings. A callout for yoga, meditation, Reiki, or Tai Chi instructors will surely yield results and they can help make these moments the start of a deeper relationship to health and wellness for the community you engage.

Movement is a medicine for creating change in a person's physical, emotional, and mental states.
—Carol Welch-Baril, neuromuscular therapist

Music is gathering. Taking our scattered thoughts and senses and coalescing us back into our core. Music is powerful.
—*Jane Siberry, singer + songwriter*

Ingredient: Music and Sounds

"Music has charms to soothe the savage breast." While we agree with William Congreve's sentiments here, our love for music tells us music and sound also touch, lift, and inspire people in ways the spoken word cannot. You can change the rhythm and flow of a meeting with deft use of music and sounds during your meetings and events.

There are beautiful ways to infuse music and sounds into meetings and gathering to significant effect. Some of our favorites are listed below.

Use a gong or chime to call the room to silence. It helps to ask the audience to quickly end their conversations when they hear the first gong or chime. By the second sounding, anyone needing to complete their conversation should be speaking in a hushed tone, and by the third and final gong, the room should be totally silent. This is so calming and pleasant compared to trying to speak over the voices, clink on glasses, and having to repeatedly ask for quiet.

Before the meeting begins, play neutral or upbeat music or songs that have some meaning to your audience. This practice also helps ensure the sound system is up and working before it is needed by the emcee.

If your meeting can benefit by using sound or music, use it. A fitting example is when doing a skills refresher for CPR, play the Bee Gees song "Stayin' Alive" as its beat is just the right timing for doing the necessary chest compressions.

Music can also be used to help people learn more about each other. You can honor and recognize special people at the meeting by playing their favorites or requests.

Using music as a way to build relationships at meetings to a high level, we have a fabulous example from the Rotary Club of Oakland. Sean Marx, CEO of Give Something Back, club president for 2017-2018, shared his love of music with the club by conducting a regular musical member engagement experience.

From the podium, he played music while displaying a playlist of songs next to the pictures of six Rotarians (called Ro-Tune-ians) on the screen. He then invited everyone to guess which Rotarian matched the featured song list. After a name was suggested by a member, Sean would poll the audience to see who agreed with the guess. After a couple of wrong guesses and some playful banter, a correct guess would emerge. Sean then promised to buy the winner a drink at the next Cocktails with the President event. It was a wonderful way to have a musical interlude at a Rotary meeting, and it was an even better way for Rotary members to get to know each other through music.

Allow music to lift your meetings to new heights and move the hearts of all who hear that call.

To me, music is a connector.
—Anna Maria Chávez, Chief Executive Officer
of the Girls Scouts of the USA

Punctuality is the soul of business.
—*Thomas C. Haliburton, politician + author*

Ingredient: Time, Timers, Timekeepers

Have you ever seen a person sitting in the front row, or maybe off to the side, who holds up a sign with a number on it—then looks for the nod of acknowledgment from the speaker? We look for those people at meetings and conferences. They matter. Beyond keeping the meeting on track, the presence of timers and timekeepers allows everyone else to relax and not stress.

Having visible timers and proactive time-keepers dramatically reduces the likelihood of having panelists and presenters run amok with their remarks which can toss your agenda to the wind. If you've ever been the speaker at a conference—where time, timers, and timekeepers aren't given their proper place of honor—you know the stress of trying to mentally rewrite and shorten your remarks as your time is eaten up. You may also know the stress of being in the audience, knowing you need to make a call, leave early, take some medication, or attend to a health-related matter in a specific time window, but now the meeting is so off the agenda you must make some tough or awkward choices.

Meetings are made much better when time and timekeepers are honored and respected. When time is masterfully managed, the content can be delivered as it was envisioned by the planners, the presenters are supported in being clear and focused, and the participants can best manage their range of physical, mental, and emotional needs.

There are several ways to effectively and thoroughly integrate time and timekeepers at your events. Some favorites include:

- Ask the audience for their help in keeping everything on time and on track.

- Expressly point out the clocks, timers, and timekeepers.

- Ask everyone to synchronize their watches, timers, etc., so everyone is using the same base time.

- Ensure speakers and presenters are in sync with the timekeepers and can communicate changes during the meeting. Whether it's done verbally, with hand signals, signage, or via text, make sure you are ready to deal with time changes on the spot.

- Ensure your designated timekeepers are ready to use the app or timer properly before they are expected to do it at the meeting.

For meetings with lots of group engagement, table talking, or if the space is quite large, it helps to have a visible and physically active way to engage the crowd in supporting good time management.

To actively engage the audience in time management, the facilitator should clearly explain and demonstrate a visual gesture she or he will make to signal that time is up and that it's time to get quiet and move on to the next portion of the day.

Example:

- When the facilitator's arms are raised in the air (like a touchdown signal at a football game) it means it's time to quiet down, wrap up the conversation, and refocus.

- As soon as you see the facilitator is in the touchdown position, EVERYONE who can should put their arms in touchdown position. This signals their understanding the room is transitioning to quiet and we need to focus on the facilitator.

- By the time the facilitator's arms are in the T position, more than half the room should be in silence and have their arms raised.

- When the facilitator's arms come down to the sides of their body it means the room should be silent and everyone should be ready to resume the meeting.

Being masterful in time management is a tragically undervalued skill. Whether it's a planning team of two people sitting next to each other, or multiple teams scattered across the country, helping your people to be powerful in time management is a superb endeavor.

Either you run the day, or the day runs you.
—Jim Rohn, author + motivational speaker

True leadership often happens with the smallest acts, in the most unexpected places, by the most unlikely individuals.
—Michelle Obama, First Lady of the United States, 2009 – 2017

Ingredient: Cultivate Leadership

Whenever you bring people together to interact, there will be opportunities for people to learn, grow, and assume leadership positions. Providing leadership development opportunities will make your meetings much more desirable for people looking to develop those skills.

A straightforward way to infuse leadership skills and opportunities into your gatherings is to appoint people to serve as group leaders or leaders for their area. These newly-appointed leaders should be able to help their group by providing instructions (printed and spoken aloud to the group) so every participant in their group has ample opportunity to participate to their best ability.

For the rest of the meeting or engagement, you should refer to these leaders with their title. Your goal is to help people assume leadership roles and help them gain experience leading a group. It is incredibly valuable to offer these opportunities to people who would not otherwise have the chance to build these skills and muscles. This includes not only students, interns, volunteers, and people who are new to your group or organization, but it also includes people who are more shy or introverted. This group can be less likely to sign up for formal leadership training and they may have jobs that don't require or foster their leadership skills.

Your printed instructions should remind the group leaders of what to say to the people in their group to keep the process moving forward smoothly.

Beyond providing clarity about the group's instructions, they should be ready to remind the group about the time they have to complete tasks, ensure every person in the group is actively engaged and participating, make sure all of the tools or supplies being used in the group are kept together, and the group is prepared to present or do the action requested of the group.

The printed instructions should also thank the group leaders for stepping up and assuming a leadership role at the meeting. Be sure to thank and acknowledge all the group leaders as a team when their task has been completed.

The leadership development virtuous cycle to embrace is:

- Create the opportunity for leaders to step up.
- Provide the tools and support for them to do it well.
- Identify and acknowledge them for taking on the leadership role.
- Repeat this cycle, actively looking to expand your reach, and strengthen your leadership-building chops.

The world needs more people who see themselves as leaders in their communities, who are willing to raise their hands up and step up into leadership roles.

Having your meetings and gatherings be a safe place where diverse leaders are developed and helped to flourish is a service to society.

Leadership is hard to define and
good leadership even harder.
—*Indra Nooyi, Chairwoman + Chief Executive*
Officer of PepsiCo

Change is the end result of all true learning.
—Leo Buscaglia, author

Ingredient: New Skills
Development

Imagine what it would mean for your team and your chosen audiences if they felt your meetings were a brilliant training ground. If your tribe becomes more skilled with every meeting, whatever else is accomplished, it's a win!

There are some skills important to your team and the communities you convene directly related to your field of interest. For emergency preparedness professionals, their audiences need to know several things. For example, how to program In Case of Emergency (ICE) contacts in a cell phone; how to use a fire extinguisher (remember the acronym PASS: P=Pull the pin, A=Aim at the base of the fire, S=Squeeze the handle, S=Sweep in a side to side motion) or how to respond properly to an earthquake, by learning to *Drop* (to the ground), take *Cover* (under sturdy furniture), and *Hold On* (to a heavy piece of furniture).

There is a whole world of skills that are great to have, fun to share, and they are easy for a group to learn together.

As educators and veterans of many classes, seminars, trainings, and educational programs, we've taught and learned many skills—some in as little as 10 minutes, several in less than an hour, and countless skills and abilities can be learned in just a few hours.

If you are regularly convening the same group of people, you can design skill sets and abilities most helpful to them in achieving their goals, which will make your meeting a hardship to miss.

Depending on how much time you have and the resources at your disposal, here are some awesome skills to instill in your tribe:

- How to use various apps on a cell phone
- Basic self-defense tactics
- How to take better pictures and videos using your phone
- Deep breathing
- Very basic graphic recording
- How to remember names quickly
- How to direct traffic in an emergency

All the above skills can be demonstrated and practiced in under 15-20 minutes. Several can be learned from watching good videos. The important thing about turning your attendees into a learning community is to consistently offer interesting, well-presented, and useful skills.

When your agenda can support a longer learning session of at least 45 minutes to an hour a beautiful skill to learn is how to create a SoulCollage® card, a fun and holistic activity that offers profound personal insights. Porcia is a trained SoulCollage® Facilitator. She has led highly engaging group activities inspired by SoulCollage® for networking, branding, and goal setting.

If members of the group have the expertise and the ability to teach a new skill, invite them to lead a class or learning session. It's a magical thing to create and nurture a learning community.

Learning is a treasure that will
follow its owner everywhere.
—Chinese Proverb

Hard skills are the foundation of a successful career. But soft skills are the cement.
—Peggy Klaus, author + executive coach

Ingredient: Soft Skills

Ensuring participants are heard and included requires planners and facilitators to broaden their perception of the essential skills their teams must possess to pull off a successful meeting. Your meeting implementation team and attendees will be well served by the influence of people who have essential soft skills and are committed to making the meeting experience great. Soft skills in this context can be any skills or talents adding value to meetings and they don't have to be job or position related. They are often categorized as interpersonal skills but are much more nuanced than this label allows.

Take out a list of your participants and consider which ones have valuable soft skills. No matter their position or level of seniority, the people with these skills should be deployed at meetings and other gatherings for optimal results.

What skills should you look for? Some of the most important ones include:

Graciousness

Some people are naturally warm, inviting, and gracious. These skilled individuals put people at ease while making people feel safe and welcomed. It's easier for an attendee to see the good and overlook the less-than-stellar moments when graciousness abounds. A meeting in which you experience noticeable courtesy stands out as memorable in the best way.

Your most gracious people are well suited to the role of the lead greeter. They can be asked to make key introductions of speakers to hosts, link presenters to technical support, and be on hand to answer questions, field criticisms, and check in with attendees. They may also be the best at leading the customer service mini-training for event greeters, volunteers, and registration staff to ensure graciousness permeates all aspects of the event.

Resourcefulness

Another critical soft skill is resourcefulness. The more important the meeting and the more people and moving parts there are to deal with, the more you'll appreciate having a resourceful person on hand. Resourceful people can create, find, and implement solutions while most others are still staring blankly at the problem.

At meetings, events, and other gatherings, the unexpected will happen. Things will fall apart. People will drop the ball. When these things happen, the presence of calm and resourceful people will keep the event on track. Making an assistant of your most resourceful team member can make a good meeting great and may turn a potential disaster into a humorous (and heroic) anecdote.

Positivity

A relentlessly positive person can help transform almost any situation. These are the people who bring the silver lining to encircle any cloud. They are the human antidotes to the Donnie and Debbie Downers of the world. Their influence can bring a smile to the face of the most dedicated cynic. When things are going great, the persistently positive people help spread the cheer far and wide. When things could be better, they show us where to find the redeeming qualities in the situation and save us from feelings of total failure.

Positive people are excellent assets on a planning team and are invaluable when it comes to implementation. Attitudes are contagious, so position your purveyors of positivity where they can achieve maximum influence. If your radiantly positive people also happen to have public speaking skills and stage presence, thank the meeting gods for this great blessing and invite those people on stage.

We think of these three soft skills—graciousness, resourcefulness, and positivity—as a Tactical Trio for creating successful meetings. They may be tricky to define in a job description, but you know them when you see them.

If you know how to identify and best utilize these soft skills, your chances of having a gratifying gathering are great.

It's all attitude. Attitude, attitude, attitude.
—Iris Apfel, American fashion icon

I realize that humor isn't for everyone.
It's only for people who want to
have fun, enjoy life, and feel alive.
—Anne Wilson Schaef, author + seminar leader

Ingredient: Humor

Few things bond an audience like good humor and, contrary to what some grumpy people believe, research shows humor helps with learning. Deployed effectively—and with caution to be appropriate, respectful and inclusive to all—humor adds to the learning environment in many ways.

Humor can reduce anxiety, boost participation, and increase motivation to focus on the material. As you may have already guessed, educators who infuse humor and fun into the learning experience are rated significantly higher by their students than those who don't.

Some people in your community are naturally funny and humorous. This should be considered an excellent asset. If you or the key people on your team aren't blessed with a sense of humor that translates well to your targeted audiences or the venues and events you hold, worry not! Fortunately, humor can be learned, bought, rented, and borrowed to make your meetings roar with laughter.

It may seem ambitious to take on learning how to amuse and delight a crowd with humor, but you may have people who've always wanted to try their hand at it, and this could be the excuse they need to finally try. You could also bring in a teacher who specializes in improvisation and stand-up comedy to help your team find and flex their funny bones. Whether they get good enough to deliver humor at your meetings isn't the point. It's a skill worthy of cultivating and nurturing.

A quick Google search will reveal the many ways humor can be bought, borrowed, or rented. There are companies who specialize in providing content for groups, companies, and major corporations because humor is a very popular topic.

YouTube is filled with free funny videos on any number of different subjects. You can find material that fits just about any niche subject and any specialized audience. Whether your audience is filled with architects, engineers, clergy, doctors, people with disabilities, musicians, animal lovers, vegans, or whomever—there is funny material already available to add humor and laughter to your gatherings.

There are clear benefits to intentionally curating a collection of related humor to delight your audiences and make your meetings memorable, meaningful and unmissable.

Humor is mankind's greatest blessing.
—*Mark Twain, author + humorist*

*If you really want to make a friend, go to some-
one's house and eat with him ... the people who
give you their food give you their heart.*
—*Cesar Chavez, labor leader + co-founder of
National Farm Workers Association*

Ingredient: Food and
Beverages

You or someone you know can probably recount a time when the food or food service at a meeting negatively overshadowed an event. Food that's late, bad, inappropriate, insufficient, visually unappetizing, cold when it was meant to be hot, difficult to serve—any of these things—can turn an otherwise normal audience into a hungry and hostile mob.

How do you think your attendees would react to a half-day morning meeting without coffee service? Seriously? It's ugly. Caffeine withdrawal isn't a good group activity, and it's detrimental to your meeting's energy and harmony. Ditto for not having plenty of drinking water for your attendees.

Appropriate food and water aren't just nice to have, they are necessities. As you should be suspecting by now, in the *Gatherings for Greatness* framework, food and beverages can be turned into spectacular, engaging, and community-building experiences.

Even if you already have wonderful food and beverages, you can still elevate your meeting game with food. For the truly committed and high achievers among you (and you know who you are), here's how you can help your participants to manage their health, diets, and comfort levels while impressing the heck out of people whose food needs are a major source of stress or anxiety. Consider providing some or all of the following items to delight your attendees whose dietary needs are an important consideration.

- A menu in advance with ingredients listed
- Labels for all dishes
- A list of ingredients for each dish served
- Special menu options by request
- A wide variety of condiments
- Diet-specific options and labels (Paleo, Keto, Gluten-Free, etc.)
- Contact info for the catering service, should there be anyone with a specific allergy or other questions

For some people, the only thing they have full control over in the actual meeting is the food.

If you have control over what is served, and how it is prepared and presented, you can WOW your crowd with foods that honor or acknowledge something meaningful to your group. Here are some examples:

- If your meeting is about local issues, you can choose locally grown, locally sourced foods, and highlight their source, and point the spotlight on those businesses to your audience.

- For a meeting touching on issues of ethnic diversity, you can feature foods representing certain regions or cultures. If the people attending represent that level of diversity, you could ask them to help you ensure the authenticity of the food.

- If you want to proudly proclaim your meeting is intentionally green or gentle on the environment you could eliminate all plastic water bottles entirely. Serve water in pitchers or dispensers and encourage people (in the invitations and reminders) to bring their own thermos or reusable drinking container. If you sell these items, make sure that's known.

Alternatively, you can give them away with your name, logo, or website imprinted on it, or affix a branding sticker or label to it. This could also be a partner contribution or a sponsorship opportunity.

- Another anti-waste low-cost/high-return action is to always bring ziptop bags when food is served at your events. If you are really going for zero waste, all edible food should be used. If the participants can't eat it all or take it with them, be ready to call the organizations who take food leftovers or make sure it goes to a local shelter.

- If you serve alcohol at your gathering, you should absolutely have a wide variety of non-alcoholic beverages displayed prominently. You can make your event particularly memorable to many by serving mocktails and fancifully served alcohol-free drinks. They look every bit as special as the fancy mixed drinks with alcohol, but they are both delicious and entirely alcohol-free. Offering attractive and interesting non-alcoholic drinks supports both non-drinkers and people intentionally avoiding alcohol. Your liquid refreshment station should also include flexible drinking straws, as they are important for the full inclusion of people with disabilities, young children, and attendees with certain types of dental work and related sensitivities.

- For emergency preparedness meetings, delicious dishes made from foods with a long shelf life (rice, beans, etc.) can be highlighted.

- A health-themed meeting can feature the range of super-foods and high-density nutrition foods.

The ways you can have food and beverages be the way you educate, engage, and pamper your participants is endless.

A fun, inexpensive, and tasty way to captivate the mind, heart, and sweet tooth of every attendee can be served up with some bags of mixed candies. "Sweet Words" is a happy engagement exercise that's easy and low-cost—but not necessarily low-calorie.

Get some big bags of mixed candies—Kisses, Lifesavers, $100,000 Bars, 3 Musketeers, Now and Later, M&Ms, Snickers, Smarties, Peeps, and other favorites—enough for everyone to have at least a piece or two. Cough drops and lozenges can also be included.

Have everyone pick a candy and share how the candy represents something positive about their job, a co-worker, or a project they are working on. As many times as this exercise is done, it's always inspiring to see how people always find wonderful and generous things to say. It's good to model the exercise by choosing a candy and making a simple statement following the directions. Using M&Ms as an example:

"I picked M&Ms for my team because they are marvelous, magical, and absolutely magnificent."

Some other lovely sentiments expressed:

"You've been a true Lifesaver to me."

"I so appreciate all the laughs, giggles and Snickers we've shared at work."

"I picked Now and Later because our financial services help seniors both Now and Later."

"I picked Peeps for my team because during the holiday rush when there was so much work and so many long hours, there was not a Peep of complaint and they were all so sweet."

Leading the "Sweet Words" candy engagement exercise at chambers of commerce and other networking or association meetings works well because it's a recurring group of people. It helps the group to remember something about the other members' businesses or relationships.

If it's a small group, you can have them share out loud with everyone. If the group is too large or if you don't have enough time, they can share with a partner or at their table. This is a great exercise to do near Easter or Halloween when candies are plentiful and mixed bags are on sale. You'll score extra bonus points if you remember to have a stash of sugar-free treats, so more people can participate.

When your meeting doesn't include food service at all, you can still provide mints or candies so people have something to consume. It's easy to print up tiny labels for candy packets or to serve mints with a sign or acknowledgment of some sort. For example, "Thank you for being awesome!" It's a small gesture, but it shows thought and appreciation for the people attending.

Even if you can't nourish their bodies with food and beverages, you can nourish their hearts and souls with how you offer something as simple as water.

Snack time is a great opportunity to put the right rocket fuel in your body.
—Samantha Cristoforetti, European Space Agency astronaut

Content is King but engagement is Queen,
and the lady rules the house!
—*Mari Smith, Facebook marketing expert*

Ingredient:
Table Tools and Toys

If your meeting or gathering has people sitting at tables, an easy, fun and playful addition comes in the form of table toys. Slinkys, pipe cleaners, clay, colored paper, markers, popsicle sticks, rubber bands—almost anything you can find in arts and crafts or creative toy stores—make for lively engagement before, during, and after meetings.

Table toy items can be left on the table for people to enjoy or you could incorporate them into the purpose of the meeting. You can give attendees some time as a group to come up with a mascot for their project or team or task them to create a project update using the items. If you have sufficient supplies, you can have everyone create something.

Depending on how large your group is, how much time you have, and how much of these supplies you have on hand, you can divide the attendees into teams, giving each team an equal amount of the items. Then, you ask them to create something using all the pieces and set a time limit.

Like the TV cooking shows where contestants have the same ingredients but create wildly different results, this toy engagement activity provides a fun and fascinating way to watch the individual and team dynamics, as well as to see the different types of skills that are present in your group.

The goal is to give people a way to creatively engage and interact. If much of your crowd enthusiastically dives into this activity, have someone from the table share aloud about their creation. This is a wonderful way for shy people or newcomers to show a talent and play a more active role in a meeting.

Besides actively engaging hands and minds, these small toys and the act of playing together often becomes an easy opening for light-hearted interpersonal conversations. Many people stay glued to their cell phones, hardly making eye contact or conversation with other meeting attendees. Others can sit and play with fidget spinners all day, driving their seat neighbors to distraction. Table toys are a welcomed alternative for many people and the people around them.

Incorporating table toys is meant to be light and fun and filled with color, texture, and creativity. Don't let any design competitions become too serious, and encourage everyone to play—including senior management.

Many times, this engagement unveils hidden talents and mad skills to be cheered and celebrated.

> *Creativity is connected to your passion,*
> *that light inside you that drives you.*
> *—Amy Poehler, actress + comedian*

*The manner of giving is worth
more than the gift.*
—*Pierre Corneille, French dramatist*

Ingredient:
Your SWAG Bag

Carefully considered, multi-purpose, attractive corporate or branded SWAG is easily one of the best ways to create a unified look and sense of team. Companies spend billions of dollars to put their names and logos on items. Some are brilliant and useful—Sharpie markers, Post-it Notes, flashlights, and multitools with rulers, wrenches, blades, and bottle openers, just to name a few. Others have limited use and can irritate consumers by being a wasted item that goes straight to landfills - like so many foam fingers do.

Most companies simply hand out the goodies. With just a bit of effort, you can make your SWAG a source of pride and joy for your participants. Don't worry if you don't have branded SWAG, it's easy and low-cost to get stickers or customized address labels to brand whatever giveaways you can afford.

The key to making SWAG memorable is to first ensure the items you stock and giveaway are useful items. No matter how much sentiment and good vibes you infuse into certain items, it's not going to make them useful or something your team and attendees will carry with them.

The next step is to create a fun and memorable way to have people put them to use. It's easy to use Post-it Notes for sending good thoughts and well wishes to colleagues. At a celebratory moment—perhaps someone's anniversary or promotion—have everyone take branded Post-it Notes and write something nice to the honoree. It could be in the form of recognition or thanks, congratulatory or complimentary, or a simple wish for continued success. The person being celebrated will end up with lots of lovely expressions—all on your company's branded Post-it Notes.

We are both particularly experienced with SWAG related to emergency preparedness. Whistles are a brilliant piece of SWAG. Few SWAG items provide as much value for such low cost and they have the added values of being small and portable with no expiration date. In handing out whistles, everyone gets the basic training for the safety code (1 blow = Yes, 2 blows = No, 3 blows = Help!), they are shown how to use it to communicate when their voices may not be audible over noises and sirens, and they are reminded of the wisdom of putting it on a keychain, a zipper pull on a sweatshirt, etc.

In some gatherings, when each person gets their own whistle, they are told whistles are the life-saving tools of the everyday hero. Every superhero has special tools—Wonder Woman has the Lasso of Truth; Thor has a hammer; Batman and Batwoman both have utility belts filled with tools to save the day. We remind them community heroes carry whistles. Everyday heroes use whistles to warn their friends and neighbors of danger, signal for help when danger is present, or to communicate over the sounds of crisis. Then, they are thanked for being a hero. For some people, it's the first time they've ever thought of themselves as being heroic. For others, it's the first time safety was made so personal to them.

There are a few universal aspirations. We all wish to be seen in the best possible light. We all wish we will emerge as heroes and do the right thing in whatever circumstance we face. Whatever your SWAG, find its highest and best purpose and give people the experience of it being awarded to them. It's worth the effort to find an item that creates a visible, emotional, and tangible connection to their higher selves.

> *Gift giving is a true art.*
> —*Vera Nazarian, author*

Tell me, and I will forget. Show me, and I may remember. Involve me, and I will understand.
—Confucius, Chinese philosopher

Ingredient: Games

Most people love to play games. Board games, trivia games, word games—they all have their ardent admirers. It would be quite a feat to have your team combine their love of games with their passion for your group's efforts. While it could involve a significant time commitment to do a fully customized version of a popular game, the results could be used in small segments as well as in a longer session.

We both watch the TV show Jeopardy, where answers are provided and the contestants compete to provide the correct question. To do your version of Jeopardy, people with knowledge (or the desire to learn) about your company, group, or initiative would need to create the answers and a corresponding list of the correct questions. It takes time to pull it all together and you'll need someone to play the Alex Trebek role, but it results in a fun way to engage people in learning and knowing more about what you want them to care about.

Other games readily lend themselves to the creation of personalized games, such as Family Feud, Trivial Pursuit, Pictionary, Cranium, Charades, and Draw Something. And, of course, you could make up your own original game.

Beyond the fun to be had playing the completed game, all the things created for these games become absolutely exquisite eye-catching fodder for social media posts, newsletters, promotions, and presentations. If you have a social media manager, they would vote for a game to be created just to get the incredible amount of social media content from it.

The people doing all the creation of the game, as well as all the people playing or watching, get to think, learn, and bond over your group, company, or initiative.

We think that's a game worth playing.

> *Life is more fun if you play games.*
> —*Roald Dahl, author*

When you know better, you do better.
—Maya Angelou, author + civil rights activist

Ingredient: Harvesting Brilliance

One of the better uses of meeting time is to harvest the ideas, opinions, and feedback from the participants, and capture it in a meaningful way. One of the best ways to do this is with a simple Post-it Note. We both swoon over the utility of these sticky jewels and we wonder what we did before the 3M Company created these little miracles.

Incorporating Post-it Note activities in your meeting serves multiple purposes. First, Post-it Notes provide an incredibly fast, easy, and accessible way to gather immediate feedback on a process, project, or initiative. Place different ideas or possibilities on the wall and give everyone some Post-its and have them write some feedback or make a request and stick it on the corresponding wall.

Some groups prefer to use online evaluations and surveys as their way of pulling in knowledge from their community. If you've trained your people to be highly responsive online, that is awesome, but most online surveys and evaluations don't consistently pull in that level of response. Post-it Note engagement offers a level of immediate action and interaction email does not provide.

Second, Post-it Notes are brilliant at helping people learn skills. Ana-Marie uses them to teach audiences how to create nuanced timelines for project management. It's easy. Just pick a project with a 4-hour timed deadline. Give everyone a pad of Post-it Notes. Designate a spot in the room for each hour. Ask people to write down what they think needs to happen in each of the four hours. Collect all the Post-its for each hour. Then, as a team, group and cluster similar comments, putting unnecessary or unfeasible actions in a designated space labeled as the "parking lot" for later consideration. Then, again as a team, put the actions in time order.

Done correctly, everyone in the group will have had the opportunity to think, move, contribute, and be part of the group process. Plus, everyone will have a far better sense of how to construct a nuanced timeline which incorporates the wisdom of the crowd. This is a great skill to cultivate.

Using our Post-it Note planning process allows managers to learn a lot about each member of the team. In some cases, it will reveal some useful soft skills—like who is good at seeing patterns, who cheers and acknowledges others, who has good handwriting, as well as who deciphers bad handwriting easily. Similarly, it can reveal some areas where additional training and caution is needed.

A caring and social use for Post-it Notes comes with sending get well, condolence, or congratulatory cards to members of your community. Rather than sending a card around and hoping it gets returned with all the signatures, you can give out colorful oversized Post-its. Have people write messages (or draw pictures) and sign their names on the Post-it. Then, simply collect them for the card or poster.

There are many other ways to harvest the individual and collective wisdom at your gathering. Much of the success of these methods depends on the size and make up of your crowd, as well as how you deploy the following techniques.

- Task someone to conduct a verbal poll or seek the insights you are looking for. People will often say what they wouldn't take the time to write. The note taker can use prefab forms, a tablet, or their phone to capture the intel.
- Designate a computer for attendees to leave their thoughts.
- Offer a prize to be given to someone who provides the answers, guidance, feedback, or comments you seek.
- Go old school and leave a suggestion box with paper for people to share their thoughts. Post the issue you want their comments on next to the box. People will often write what they wouldn't say aloud.

Harvesting the wisdom, insights, and brilliance of your assembled tribe reaps a multitude of rewards. It can be especially useful when you seek solutions to problems, honest feedback on issues, or when it truly matters to create a nuanced and sensitive response to an issue.

How many times have you seen an ad campaign or company promotion resulting in swift and harsh public condemnation as soon as it was released? It appeared they didn't receive any honest feedback from anyone outside their paid bubble.

Don't be that company. Help your people to learn, think, and regularly harvest that brilliance.

I have great belief in the power of community.
—Terry Tempest Williams, author +
conservationist

Either you follow up or you fold up.
—Bernard Kelvin Clive, author + brand
strategist

Ingredient: Follow-Up
Actions

There is no shortage of business consultants who preach about the importance of following up in the sales cycle. Business publications routinely publish listicles detailing the top however-many reasons why following up is critical in sales, customer service, and business development. While follow-up is understood and accepted in those areas of business, it's not so well understood or valued in the context of meetings, gatherings, or some events.

Both of us ran nonprofit organizations and we both plead guilty to not doing nearly the level of follow-up to meetings and events that we know would have been helpful. Quality follow-up takes time, energy, and other resources that neither of us had.

Like the ingredient of initiating pre-meeting huddles and trainings, follow-up action also tends to get shortchanged in the glory and gushing praise department. It would be a mistake to underestimate the incredible power and value of targeted follow-up.

If you are reading this book because you are looking to change the status quo or seeking to make a ruckus to change the world for the better, you can't afford to not do intentional follow-up.

Following up powerfully so your attendees derive maximum benefit from having participated, is a skill bordering on an art form. Much of the brilliance of good follow-up is created in the foundation of the actual meeting. Some pieces worthy of including:

- Good note-taking makes sending your post-event information easier and faster.
- A skilled facilitator who clarifies points during the meeting helps eliminate post-meeting confusion.
- Instilling the habit of always having a "parking lot" so off topic or interesting and potentially important (but not urgent enough to be addressed now) issues have a place to live.
- For a recurring group, having an online calendar where reminders can be set,

deadlines posted, and future meeting dates shared, makes a dramatic difference.

- A Google Doc accessible by all can become a post-meeting destination location and preferred resource and repository of the meeting's key elements.

Exquisitely done follow-up makes it exponentially more likely your attendees can take action on the key issues of the meeting. Well-crafted notes sent soon after the meeting allow absent people to stay informed and attendees to take action. A shared calendar and Google Doc can create easy and ongoing access for people looking to fully embrace the meeting and its goals.

If your normal follow-up is in the form of post-meeting evaluations or surveys and you get a good response rate, yay for you! Many meetings have no follow up to speak of. However, a different kind of follow up is needed if you are truly looking to create something great from your meetings and this type of follow-up brings something more precious than evaluations.

We recommend following up with a single-minded goal of finding and deeply connecting with your true champions, kindred spirits, and passion partners. If you create a good meeting and you bring the right people to it you are just about guaranteed to find people who will come again, show interest, and want to be on your mailing list. That's great! Bravo, and well-done. Really, it's a wonderful thing and a fine result.

Tracking down true believers, empowered advocates, and people with a shared passion for your message and vision reaps rewards, opens doors, and builds for the future in ways which will change the trajectory of your efforts.

If you are given the choice between doing follow-up activities to yield 100 new people on your mailing list who think your meeting was great or doing follow-up activities to produce 10 people who see and champion your vision and are willing to join you in your pursuit, there is really very little choice. One is a happy consumer of your services and the other is the missing link in crossing the chasm and fulfilling on your vision. If you are building a movement, you need these passionate believers.

Two straight-up recommendations for virtually all meeting conveners is to get the audience to do two things before they walk out: 1) Make a commitment about their next steps, which you will capture. 2) Ask the attendees to self-identify their level of interest in working with you and their preferred type of follow up.

Post-it Notes can be used to capture this intel as could providing a number to text the information to. Of course, standard ways of capturing this information (notes, snail mail, emails, and web messages) can also be welcomed.

Getting this type of specific intel from your audience BEFORE they leave your meeting will give you the ability to inquire about their own actions, next steps, and promises.

This beats the socks off trying to create and deploy a survey about your attendees' intentions. Finding out—in the moment—directly from your targets, how interested and committed they are to connecting more deeply is truly a time-, money-, and energy-saving blessing. From this you find your tribe, you know who's your ride or die, and you build your posse.

Given the level of results you can achieve by embracing this kind of follow-up, frankly, we think it deserves far bigger props. Far. Bigger.

The world is full of willing people,
some willing to work, the rest willing to let
them.
—Robert Frost, poet

Let us proudly be the crazy ones, the ambitious ones, the ones who see beyond the limits of today, who capture the opportunities, who find the resources that will build a better tomorrow, not for ourselves, but for those depending upon us to get it right.
—Ertharin Cousin, Executive Director of the United Nations World Food Programme, 2012-2017

Epilogue

We started this book with a shared belief that bringing people together is a noble undertaking. The people who take on this endeavor are the quiet catalysts behind great innovation and needed social change. The power of masterful meetings and game-changing gatherings is so terribly misunderstood, and this is a gross waste of time, money, and human potential. We were both reared with the "waste not, want not" mentality, so with this book we aspire to both stop the waste and start a meeting revolution.

You'd think reframing meetings so that the wants, needs, desires, and concerns of the target audience take center stage is an obvious thing to do. But it isn't. Even as true believers of this approach, and as long-time conveners and producers of a wide array of meetings and gatherings for diverse audiences, we were surprised by how much we got out of fully embracing these 24 ingredients in the writing of this book.

This book was written over many months with many one-on-one meetings. We met in each other's homes, in coffee shops, Elks Clubs, restaurants, libraries, and wherever Wi-Fi, relative quiet, and clean bathrooms could be found. We brought our tools and props (notes, books, printouts, and more) so we could fully immerse ourselves, and make the physical environment support our needs.

We are both crazy proud and impressed by how great it felt to add movement to our writing routine. We set a timer so every hour we'd remember to do some stretching, brain exercises, vigorous movement, and sometimes a 60-second plank.

We regularly harvested the brilliance of our extended community — whether friend, family, housemate, spouse, house pet, guest, barista, or stranger — if they were in our physical or mental space, we drew from them and welcomed their wisdom. We had brief pre-meeting huddles, took the time to dictate notes for follow-up, and assigned tasks based on our time, schedules, and talents.

We shared music, food, resources, apps, and insights regularly, and we let our quirks and idiosyncrasies bring joy and inspiration. At Ana-Marie's house, we passed a Seth Godin action figure around. It's NIB (new, in box) and overlooks her desk. She's hoping to get it autographed one day. At Porcia's house, we strike the Wonder Woman pose, under the Wonder Woman card overlooking her desk. We are also proud Instant Potters, having savored many incredible meals cooked in the new must-have Instant Pot Ana-Marie introduced to Porcia.

Though we have been friends and colleagues for years, we learned so much about each other and we had a great time using this content in our two-person book writing meetings.

We hope you will have as wonderful an experience coming together to discuss how you will create meetings and gatherings to bring out the best in your audiences. We wish for you to use the ingredients herein with joy and reverence for the opportunity you have to change lives by reimagining the beautiful act of bringing people together. And, our greatest aspiration is that you will go forth and create meetings that make the world a better place.

Thank you so much for choosing to explore the *Gatherings for Greatness* approach. If we can help you make your meetings matter more and bring greatness to your gatherings, just reach out.

With heaps of gratitude, Ana-Marie and Porcia

My Story
by Ana-Marie Jones

I'm a born-and-raised New Yorker, with twenty-nine years of California living so far and currently loving Oakland.

The domestic research division of the American Association of Advertising Agencies (AAAA) provided my first ten years of full-time employment. Having unlimited access to interesting reading materials (all about advertising and marketing) never got old. I remain endlessly fascinated by human nature and how we can channel it to serve the greater good. If you've seen my presentations on the marketing of emergency management, this is where that particular nerd's-eye view was cultivated.

My first emergency management job came when I was three and a half years old. My parents told me I was getting a baby sister (Lisa) and my job was to keep her safe. I hopped aboard the big sister responsibility train and never looked back.

In 1989, I moved to San Francisco and the Loma Prieta earthquake struck. Boy, howdy! After growing up seeing safety and readiness as loving and positive acts, I found it tough to encounter fear, threats, acronyms, bureaucracy, and overwhelming graphic content in meeting after meeting in my job at the American Red Cross. So, I embraced my nickname, Ms. Duct Tape, and set out to be a purveyor of positive preparedness and to infuse shameless optimism in all aspects of emergency management.

I still embrace my Hunter College High School motto: *Mihi cura futuri*. It means "The care of the future is mine." So, for as long as our futures include meetings, I aspire to make them awesome.

My Story
by Porcia Chen Silverberg

As a longtime champion of community service, women, and immigrants, I have built a career in creating communities of under-recognized heroes and helping them to lead their best lives. It all started with a relentless quest that included more than 20 jobs in more than 10 industries, including entertainment, gaming, publishing, telecommunications, public relations, sales, marketing, and entrepreneurship. I was even a child actress in Taiwan, where I was born.

Eventually, I found my people, my passion, and my purpose. As the Community Relations Manager at the Rocky Mountain Public Broadcasting Network (RMPBN) in Denver, Colorado, I met passionate social change agents and advocates. Like me, they longed to make a positive difference in a world filled with gaps that desperately needed closing and spirits that needed lifting. I realized playing small doesn't serve anyone. A Marianne Williamson poem inspired me to create The National Center for Community Relations, a chamber of communities connecting businesses, nonprofits, and government.

Family circumstances brought us (me, my husband, our two children, and our dogs) to California. For nine years, I served as the Executive Director of Thrive, The Alliance of Nonprofits for San Mateo County, where I continued my mission by convening and serving hundreds of organizations.

My journey from immigrant girl to where I am today was influenced so much by the many people I met along the way. And, I met most of them in meetings. For me, making meetings great is another way of serving the highest good.

Our Stories

The Pollyanna Posse Story

As we came together to write this book, we realized we had so many shared loves, odd obsessions, pet peeves, and quirks. OK, so we're a little heavy on the quirks. Don't judge. Here's a sample: We both swoon over artfully delivered emotional generosity. We both frown on gratuitous negative framing—the "for Dummies" books come to mind. The books filling our bookshelves are remarkably similar, and we LOVE libraries. We both have a greater-than-average love for Seth Godin. We think Instant Pots are magical. We binge-watch TED Talks, and when something ignites our curiosity, we tumble headlong down a research rabbit hole, smiling all the way. We are both flaming optimists, and we get teary-eyed over Mr. Rogers stories. Both of us absolutely love the character *Pollyanna**, *and we actually play the Glad Game.* We realized that we wanted to create other things together—all of them brimming with our shared enthusiasm for bringing more positivity to the world. Thus the Pollyanna Posse was born.

You hold in your hand a distillation of our lifetimes of experience and years spent helping people leverage ordinary interpersonal interactions into potentially transformative human connections. We both have the Pollyanna gene and we hope to spread that sunniness far and wide

The prospect of your benefitting from our years of trial and error, and less-than-productive time spent in past gatherings, makes us giddy with gratitude. We aspire to create other products and services to help you find more joy, love, fulfillment, and success.

* For more information about the character Pollyanna, please visit en.wikipedia.org/wiki/Pollyanna

Our Services

We offer the following services related to the content of *Gatherings for Greatness:*

- Consultations
- Facilitations
- Coaching
- Staff trainings
- Keynote presentations
- Seminars and workshops
- Webinars and conference calls

We are both experienced facilitators, and all of our services are designed to help you get more out of your meetings, gatherings, and other engagements.

To schedule a service or get more information, please contact us or visit PollyannaPosse.com.

Resources

Please note: We use Petty Link for URL shortening (https://petty.link/ref/PollyannaPosse) to prevent scam redirections, to avoid sharing dead links, and to make life easier for people using paperback or hardcover books.

Ingredient: First Things First
The Arora Collective, Fundraising for introverts and consulting for social good, http://petty.link/G4G1

Ingredient: Wisdom and Acceptance
5 Ways to Embrace Change, http://petty.link/G4G2

10 Ways to Embrace Changes, http://petty.link/G4G3

Ingredient: Naming, Framing, and Gaming You Goal
"Starting with Why," TED Talk, Simon Sinek, http://petty.link/G4G4

Ingredient: The Invitation
"Introductions," Clay Hebert, http://petty.link/G4G5

Ingredient: Physical Environment
MacGyver, a popular TV show that aired from 1985 to 1992. Learn to MacGyver anything

from a secret agent armed with almost infinite resourcefulness. http://petty.link/G4G6

Ingredient: Stories and Memorable Moments

"Made to Stick: Why Some Ideas Survive and Others Die," by Chip Heath and Dan Heath, http://petty.link/G4G7

"The Power of Moments: Why Certain Experiences Have Extraordinary Impact," by Chip Heath and Dan Heath, http://petty. link/G4G7A

Midpen Media Center Storytelling workshop, Elliot Margolis, http://petty.link/G4G8

"The Danger of A Single Story," Chimamanda Ngozi Adichie, TED Talk, http://petty.link/G4G9

Ingredient: Acknowledgment

"Everyday Leadership," Drew Dudley, TED Talk, http://petty.link/G4G10

"The Benefits of Gratitude," HuffPost, http://petty.link/G4G10A

"Validation," YouTube, http://petty.link/G4G11

Ingredient: Networking to Build a Better World
Top 10 Business Networking Groups, http://petty.link/G4G12

"Tribes: We Need You to Lead Us," by Seth Godin, http://petty.link/G4G13

"The Tribes We Lead," Seth Godin, http://petty.link/G4G13A

"An Introvert's Guide to Networking," http://petty.link/G4G14

Ingredient: Rewards, Giveaways, and Sponsored Opportunities
The Top Four Benefits of Corporate Sponsorship, http://petty.link/G4G15

Ingredient: Pre-Meeting Huddles and Trainings

"Checklist Manifesto," by Atul Gawande, http://petty.link/G4G17

Circle Communications, event curator and planner, http://petty.link/G4G18

Basic Event Planning Checklist, Marriott Hotels, http://petty.link/G4G19

Event Planning Template, Smartsheet, http://petty.link/G4G20

Ingredient: Agreements and Ground Rules

"8 Ground Rules for Great Meetings," Harvard Business Review, http://petty.link/G4G21

10 Tools For Conducting Live Polls During A Presentation, http://petty.link/G4G22

Ingredient: Stillness and Movement

Tara Brach, http://petty.link/G4G25

Laughter Yoga, Celeste Greene, http://petty.
link/G4G26

Ingredient: Music and Sounds
"Between Music and Medicine," Robert
Gupta, TED Talk, http://petty.link/G4G27

"Stayin' Alive," Bee Gees, http://petty.link/
G4G28A

"Happy," Pharrell Williams, http://petty.
link/G4G29

Ingredient: Time, Timers, Timekeepers
10 Best Online Timers, http://petty.link/G4G23

Free Insight Timer App, http://petty.link/G4G24

Free Online Timer App, http://petty.link/
G4G24A

Ingredient: Cultivate Leadership
"What It Takes to Be A Great Leader,"
Roselinde Torres, TED Talk, http://petty.
link/G4G30

"How to Start a Movement," Derek Sivers, TED Talk, http://petty.link/G4G31

"Anything You Want," by Derek Sivers, http://petty.link/G4G31A

DogWatch Navigation, executive coaching and cognitive behavioral therapy, http://petty.link/DogWatch

Ingredient: New Skills Development
"Your Body Language Shapes Who You Are," Amy Cuddy, TED Talk, http://petty.link/G4G32

"Presence: Bringing Your Boldest Self to Your Biggest Challenges," by Amy Cuddy, http://petty.link/G4G32A

The Curious Person's Guide to Learning Anything, Stephen Robinson, http://petty.link/G4G33

How to Master Any Skill, Tim Ferriss, http://petty.link/G4G33A

"Tools of Titans: The Tactics, Routines, and Habits of Billionaires, Icons, and World-Class Performers," by Tim Ferriss, http://petty.link/G4G33B

Traffic Direction, dailymotion.com/video/x2rukiq

Ingredient: Soft Skills
"Stop Calling Them Soft Skills," Seth Godin, http://petty.link/G4G35

"Soft Skills You Need," Monster.com, http://petty.link/G4G36

"Soft Skills Presentation," Richa Maheshwari, http://petty.link/G4G37

Ingredient: Humor
Joke Writing Made Simple, Greg Dean, http://petty.link/G4G38

Dry Bar Comedy, http://petty.link/G4G39

"Highly Scientific Taxonomy of Haters,"
Negin Farsad, TED Talk, http://petty.
link/G4G40

Ingredient: Food and Beverages
Mocktails, http://petty.link/G4G41

Planning Corporate Event on a Budget,
http://petty.link/G4G42

Find nonprofits to take leftover food, Call
2-1-1, 211.org, http://petty.link/G4G43

Copia, a real-time food management solu-
tion, http://petty.link/G4G44

Food Runners, http://petty.link/G4G45

Ingredient: Table Tools and Toys
Meeting Room Fidget Set, http://petty.
link/G4G46

Ingredient: Your SWAG Bag
Brand Creative, http://petty.link/G4G47

Disaster swag and products, use coupon code "MsDuctTape", http://petty.link/ReadyCare

Ingredient: Games
Create your own jeopardy game, http://petty.link/G4G48

Ingredient: Harvesting Brilliance
"The Wisdom of Crowds" by James Surowiecki, http://petty.link/G4G49

Ingredient: Follow-Up Actions
"Managing Action Items to Increase Accountability," Dana Brownlee, http://petty.link/G4G50

"How to Write a Great Follow-Up Email After a Meeting," MindMaven, http://petty.link/G4G51

Getting People to Follow Up on Action Items, http://petty.link/G4G52

For Meeting Planners and Facilitators:
Office Oxygen, http://petty.link/G4G53

Trainers Warehouse, http://petty.link/G4G54

For Aspiring Authors:
Author Academy Elite, a full-service hybrid model publisher with extraordinary leadership and integrity, an engaged community, and excellent resources and support, http://petty.link/AAE

Bestseller in a Weekend, a great step-by-step book writing program for self-motivated authors to write and self-publish their own books, http://petty.link/BSIAW

99designs, a brilliant platform with rock star customer service for crowdsourcing your design needs, http://petty.link/G4G57

Oliver Editorial Services, http://petty.link/G4G59

Additional Resources:
NPIQ, Branding and Marketing Consultants for Nonprofits, http://petty.link/G4G60

Interpro, Inc., Strategic Planning, Project Management, and Business Consulting Services, http://petty.link/G4G61

Freelance Services Marketplace, http://petty.link/G4G62

Cartoon Illustrations, http://petty.link/G4G63

Quotabelle, http://petty.link/G4G64

Goodreads, http://petty.link/G4G65

BrainyQuote, http://petty.link/G4G66

Brain Training, http://petty.link/G4G67

DepositPhotos, Royalty-Free Stock Photos, http://petty.link/G4G68

Landmark Worldwide, http://petty.link/G4G69

Instant Pot (yes, it meant that much to us,) http://petty.link/G4G70

Here's what my love affair with quotations has taught me: the more you focus on words that uplift you, the more you embody the ideas contained in those words.

—Oprah, entrepreneur + television icon

"Bringing people together is a noble undertaking!" The Pollyanna Posse

Gatherings for Greatness Quotes:

The most fulfilled people are those who get up every morning and stand for something larger than themselves.

—Wilma Mankiller

Change the way you look at things and the things you look at change.

—Wayne W. Dyer

Mobilize others with radical acts of generosity.

—Robyn Scott

You are defined by your ingredients, by the way you touch them, by the flavors you draw from them.

—Graham Elliot

The journey rarely begins the way you scripted.

—Brandi Chastain

You can have everything in life you want if you will just help other people get what they want.

—Zig Ziglar

The path to change is best traveled when we travel together.

—Sheryl Sandberg

This is the power of gathering: it inspires us, delightfully, to be more hopeful, more joyful, and more thoughtful: in a word, more alive.
— Alice Waters

A key component of wisdom is fearlessness, which is not the absence of fear, but rather not letting our fears get in the way.
— Arianna Huffington

Plan your work, and work your plan.
— Pat Summitt

If you project big goals, you may fall short, but you'll achieve more than you thought possible.
— Theresa Grentz

Who would refuse an invitation to such a shining adventure?
— Amelia Earhart

Nothing annoys people so much as not receiving invitations.
— Oscar Wilde

The ideal space must contain elements of magic, serenity, sorcery, and mystery.

—Luis Barragan

Architecture can't force people to connect, it can only plan the crossing pointes, remove barriers, and make the meeting places useful and attractive.

—Denise Scott Brown, Architect

There's always room for a story that can transport people to another place.

—J.K. Rowling

If you can tell a story well, you can move people to do something.

—Soledad O'Brien

In Acknowledgment Of Our Past, We Become Strengthened To Embrace Our Future.

—Eleesha

No one who achieves success does so without acknowledging the help of others. The wise and confident acknowledge this help with gratitude.

—Alfred North Whitehead

There are two things people want more than sex and money—recognition and praise.

—Mary Kay Ash

Personal relationships are always the key to good business. You can buy networking; you can't buy friendships.

—Lindsay Fox

I love people. Everybody. I love them, I think, as a stamp collector loves his collection. Every story, every incident, every bit of conversation is raw material for me.

—Sylvia Plath

Networking is more about "farming" than it is "hunting." It's about cultivating relationships.

—Dr. Ivan Misner

It's important to find your tribe.

—RuPaul

Give and give again. Keep hoping, keep trying, and keep giving!

—Anne Frank

Every gift which is given, even though it be small, is in reality great, if it is given with affection.

—Pindar

Just like we planned it, just like we practiced. We did it.

—Alice Bowman

With adequate planning, passion and perseverance, you can achieve the God-given goals.

—Lailah Gifty Akita

You only exist because of the agreements you made with yourself and with the other humans around you.

—José Luis Ruiz

Your life works to the degree you keep your agreements.

—Werner Erhard

It's a transformative experience to simply pause instead of immediately filling up the space.

—Pema Chodron

Movement is a medicine for creating change in a person's physical, emotional, and mental states.

—Carol Welch-Baril

Music is gathering. Taking our scattered thoughts and senses and coalescing us back into our core. Music is powerful. The first few chords can change us where no self-help books can.

—Jane Siberry

To me music is a connector.

—Anna Maria Chávez

Punctuality is the soul of business.

—Thomas C. Haliburton

Either you run the day, or the day runs you.

—Jim Rohn

True leadership often happens with the smallest acts, in the most unexpected places, by the most unlikely individuals.

—Michelle Obama

Leadership is hard to define and good leadership even harder.

—Indra Nooyi

Change is the end result of all true learning.

—Leo Buscaglia

Learning is a treasure that will follow its owner everywhere.

—Chinese Proverb

Hard skills are the foundation of a successful career. But soft skills are the cement.

—Peggy Klaus

It's all attitude. Attitude, attitude, attitude.

—Iris Apfel

I realize that humor isn't for everyone. It's only for people who want to have fun, enjoy life, and feel alive.

—Anne Wilson Schaef

Humor is mankind's greatest blessing.

—Mark Twain

If you really want to make a friend, go to someone's house and eat with him… the people
who give you their food give you their heart.
— Cesar Chavez

Snack time is a great opportunity to put the
right rocket fuel in your body.
— Samantha Cristoforetti

Content is King but engagement is Queen,
and the lady rules the house!
— Mari Smith

Creativity is connected to your passion, that
light inside you that drives you.
— Amy Poehler

The manner of giving is worth more than
the gift.
— Pierre Corneille

Gift giving is a true art.
— Vera Nazarian

Tell me, and I will forget. Show me, and I may
remember. Involve me, and I will understand.
— Confucius

When you know better, you do better.

—Maya Angelou

I have great belief in the power of community.

—Terry Tempest Williams

Either you follow up or you fold up.

—Bernard Kelvin Clive

The world is full of willing people, some willing to work, the rest willing to let them.

—Robert Frost

Let us proudly be the crazy ones, the ambitious ones, the ones who see beyond the limits of today, who capture the opportunities, who find the resources that will build a better tomorrow, not for ourselves, but for those depending upon us to get it right.

—Ertharin Cousin

God grant me the serenity to accept the things I cannot change, the courage to change the things I can and the wisdom to know the difference.

—Serenity Prayer

Our deepest fear is not that we are inadequate. Our deepest fear is that we are powerful beyond measure. It is our light, not our darkness that most frightens us.

— Marianne Williamson

Even though it's usually at the end,
the acknowledgments are often
the most important part of a book.
—Seth Godin, author + entrepreneur

Deserving of Extra Special Acknowledgments:
Ana-Marie: Lisa, Grace, Maren, Elie,
Caryl, Jared
Porcia: Mom, Cris, Aspen, Cricia, Bobby,
Kay, Patches

People Who Get a Tip of the Hat and Heart:
Ana-Marie: Angelica, Ariel, Gabriel, Galen, Andrew, Maryanne, Bill, Michael, Mikal, Rotarians, Daniel

Porcia: Alexandra, Jodi, Suzanne, Leila, Vinney, Ellen

Other Sources of Inspiration:
Pollyanna Whittier, Kary Oberbrunner, Chellie Campbell, Pam Grout, Oprah, Patricia Moreno, Seth Godin, Fred Rogers, Maya Angelou, Kamal Ravikant, Alicia Dunams, Simon Sinek, Insight Timer contributors, Brené Brown, Roxanne Gay

Places We Wrote, When Not in Our Homes:
Elks Lodges (San Francisco, Alameda, Palo Alto)
Rotary Club of Oakland #3
Bacheesos, Oakland
The Culture Collective

Made in the USA
San Bernardino, CA
10 January 2019